T0302599

Káin Ná!

/Ká·in Ná/
Let's Eat!

An Illustrated Guide to Philippine Food

Felice Prudente Sta. Maria
Bryan Koh
Illustrated by Mariel Ylagan Garcia

RPD PUBLICATIONS

Kain Na!: An Illustrated Guide to Philippine Food

The Crown Book Group, Inc.
www.thecrownbookgroup.com

First published in the Philippines in 2019 by RPD Publications
a division of The Crown Book Group, Inc.

RPD Publications
20/F, Zuellig Building, Makati Avenue corner Paseo de Roxas,
Makati City, 1225, Metro Manila, Philippines
E-mail: info@rpdpublications.com | Website: www.rpdpublications.com

ISBN: 978-621-95833-3-6

A CIP catalogue record for this book is available
from the National Library of the Philippines.

Printed in Singapore

Table of Contents

Introduction

Philippine cuisine is like no other. Endemic culinary treasures have adapted ingredients and cooking techniques from insular and continental Asia, the former Hispanic Empire of the Reformation, the United States of America when it managed colonies in the early 20th century, and the globe's post-modern flourish. Cooks around the archipelago handle the mix with increasing creative innovation.

Seeking Satisfaction

A fiesta meal is the epitome of Philippine cuisine, a history of the quest for abundant deliciousness laid out on the dining table or buffet. Whether in a Muslim or a Christian community, gold and red are the festival colors. Maguindanao feasts are eloquently poetic in their use of turmeric yellow rice symbolic of royalty and, in pagan times, the heavenly. Red is the color of blood. And during a fiesta, thoughts of the heavenly and the mortal connect.

In Christian areas, expect to find deeply flavored broths like pansit *Mólo*; several *guisádos*, stews with rich sauces golden from annatto, red from tomato, or brown from toasted breadcrumbs or soy sauce; *rellénos*, forcemeats with ground mixed meats, raisins, green olives, hardboiled eggs, ham, sausages; whole *apáhap* or *lápulápu* fish with thick, white meat made luscious by baking with olive oil in an oven or cooked in an ancient manner wrapped in leaves and baked in glowing ash. The celebrity is a spit-roasted piglet or pig that like chicken was a pre-Islamic and a pre-Christian offering to the holy unseen as one sought blessings.

For sweets, there will be usually the luscious *leche flán*, creamier than the celebrated original Spanish custard due to the latter's increased use in egg yolks. The merengue roll of *brázo de Mercedes*, the coconut cream *tibòk-tibòk* pudding, fresh ripe mangoes, carabao milk candies, and perhaps an apple pie or fruit salad bathed in thick cream are other featured dishes for the line-up.. The polite guest will have a little or, preferably, a lot of everything.

Personalizing Menus

Filipinos seem to prefer a variety of dishes served altogether at a meal. The "eat all you can buffet" satisfies the native craving and desire for variety has made the Philippine meal flexible. Even the simplest repast of rice and a tiny piece of fish has hidden complexities of savor. One is expected to be spontaneous in combining and sequencing the tastes and the flavors of every menu. Dipping sauces, relishes, pickles, mashes, sauces, gravies, vinegars, a ripe fruit on the side (often a banana or a ripe mango), fresh chili to bite on, and beverages ranging from broths to sodas are provided. Further variety is assured because textures in a meal range from very soft and creamy to crispy or hard.

Native gourmands can recognize at least eight stages in the life of a fruit: *hiláw*, unripe; *bigláw*, half-ripe; *bálok-bálok*, almost ready for removing from a tree; *hilág*, close to ripening; *manibaláng*, fruit becoming ripe; *hinóg*, ripe; *laóng*, very ripe; *lánas*, past edibleness. Artisans know which stage is best for preserving a fruit by sun-drying, packing in syrup, or pickling, and for baking into cookies or a pie.

Meals are perfect for the tropics where one must sweat to release body heat. Filipino cooks are masters in handling sourness provided by fruit pulps of *batwán*, *tábon-tábon*, *kamyás* and *sampálok* as well as tender leaves like *alibangbáng* and violet *píngol bató*. Acids in vinegars made from sugarcane, coconut, nípa, cashew, and pineapple cause a sweat. Sea salt in its natural form or as a salter in paste-like *bagoóng* and sauce-like *patís* or *tóyo* can too. One is expected to mix and match what is on the table to please fickle desires that change with every moment. The native cook will even encourage it.

Finding Joy

Eating the Filipino way, however, is not only a celebration of cooking but of how valuable relationships are with one another. "*Káin ná*" is the call to table. It means, "Let us eat now." The nationwide preference is to dine with others. Mealtime is when friends and family share happy stories, never anxieties and tragedies. An invitation to the table is often accompanied by a light tug on the arm. The lady of the home may take liberties and refill guests' plates herself as conversations liven up. A Philippine meal is incomplete without joy.

Eating and joy are so tightly linked. *Nayánayá* means serving food to others and being happy. The archaic word from central Philippines is a recipe for personal joy and harmony that result from bringing delight to others through food and beverage. Filipinos love to feed as much as they love to eat.

Menus can be curated and costly or meager with portions rationed frugally. When served with flamboyant affection, spiced with humor, and sensed as blessing, even the humblest meal becomes a feast. KÁIN NÁ! offers a sampler of what can satisfy taste buds while sealing and celebrating friendships. A wish for joy is the secret ingredient of Philippine deliciousness.

Felice Prudente Sta. Maria
Bryan Koh

Almusál

/Al·mu·sál/

Breakfast

Like their Southeast Asian neighbors, Filipinos eat what is served at other times of the day also for breakfast. Rice left over from the night before may be eaten cold or awakened by frying. New rice becomes porridge. A portable breakfast to bring into fields, on a fishing boat, even to school and work is made by boiling an individual serving of rice with a bit of protein till solid while wrapped in leaves. The wrappers are deemed folded-leaf folk art. Baked wheat breads and rice cakes steamed, boiled, or baked are convenient foods. Noodles in broths or stir-fries are also choices for starting the day.

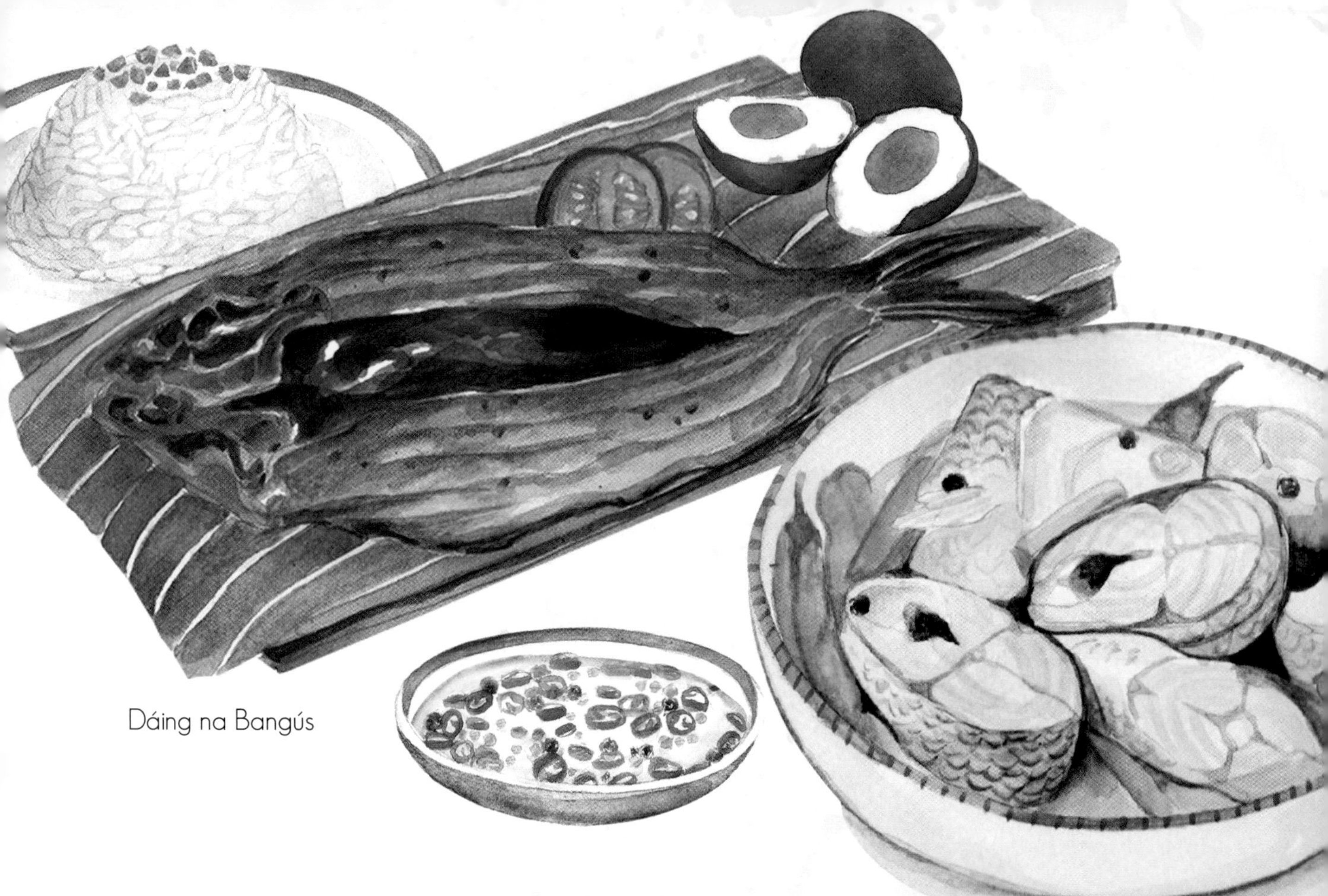

Dáing na Bangús

Paksíw na Bangús

The Breakfast Bangús

/Ba·ngús/

Paksíw na bangús (milkfish stewed in vinegar, turmeric, chili) served with white rice or fried *dáing na bangús* (milkfish cut open like a butterfly and marinated in vinegar) accompanied by garlic-flavored fried rice are typical morning fare. Salted duck egg or fried chicken egg, ripe tomato, and a dipping sauce of vinegar can be added.

Púto Máya

/Pú·to Má·ya/

Soft, unctuous grains of glutinous rice cooked in coconut milk with a little ginger are fashioned into little patties or triangular mounds that are then swaddled in banana leaf. Some are sprinkled with sesame seeds. A favorite morning meal in Cebu, *púto máya* is always paired with *sikwáte* (Cebuano chocolate drink) and sometimes eaten with ripe mango.

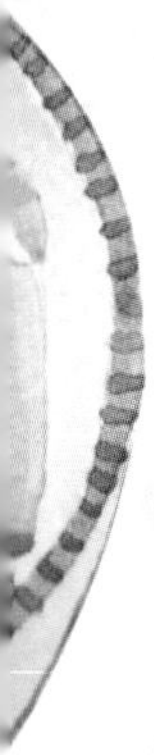

Tsamporádo

/Tsam·po·rá·do/

Tsamporádo is chocolate porridge made with native cacao (kakáw) and rice that can be glutinous if preferred. Sugar, white or brown, is cooked in or added at the table, along with carabao or cow milk too. Salted fish called *tuyó* or smoked fish called *tinapá* is sprinkled in the porridge flaked or in small pieces to balance the sweetness.

Pistú at Pán de Sál

/Pis·tú/ & /Pán de Sál/

In Pampanga, the gentry breakfast serves *pistú*, eggs scrambled lavishly with ingredients introduced during Spanish colonial times: ham, *chorízo* sausage, tomato, and potato. The breakfast bun, *pán de sál* is warmed and served with butter and local jams made of Baguio strawberry, *bignáy* berry, *kalamansî* rind, coconut, guava, mango, or Sagada orange.

Tósilóg

Tápsilóg

Tósilóg, Tápsilóg, at Lóngsilóg

/Tó·si·lóg/, /Táp·si·lóg/, & /Lóng·si·lóg/

Pink, sweet, ham-like pork *tocíno* and brown, salty, dried beef *tápa* are breakfast favorites. Regional variations of *lónganísas* (sausages) abound. Vigan's is redolent with garlic and sugarcane vinegar. Sulipan adds *dáyap* (lime) juice. Lucban puts páprikâ. Filipino humor abbreviates the menu: *tósilóg* stands for TO (*tocíno*), SI (*sinangág*, fried rice) and LÓG (*itlóg*, egg). TA in *tápsilóg* stands for *tápa* and LONG in *lóngsilóg* stands for *lónganísa*.

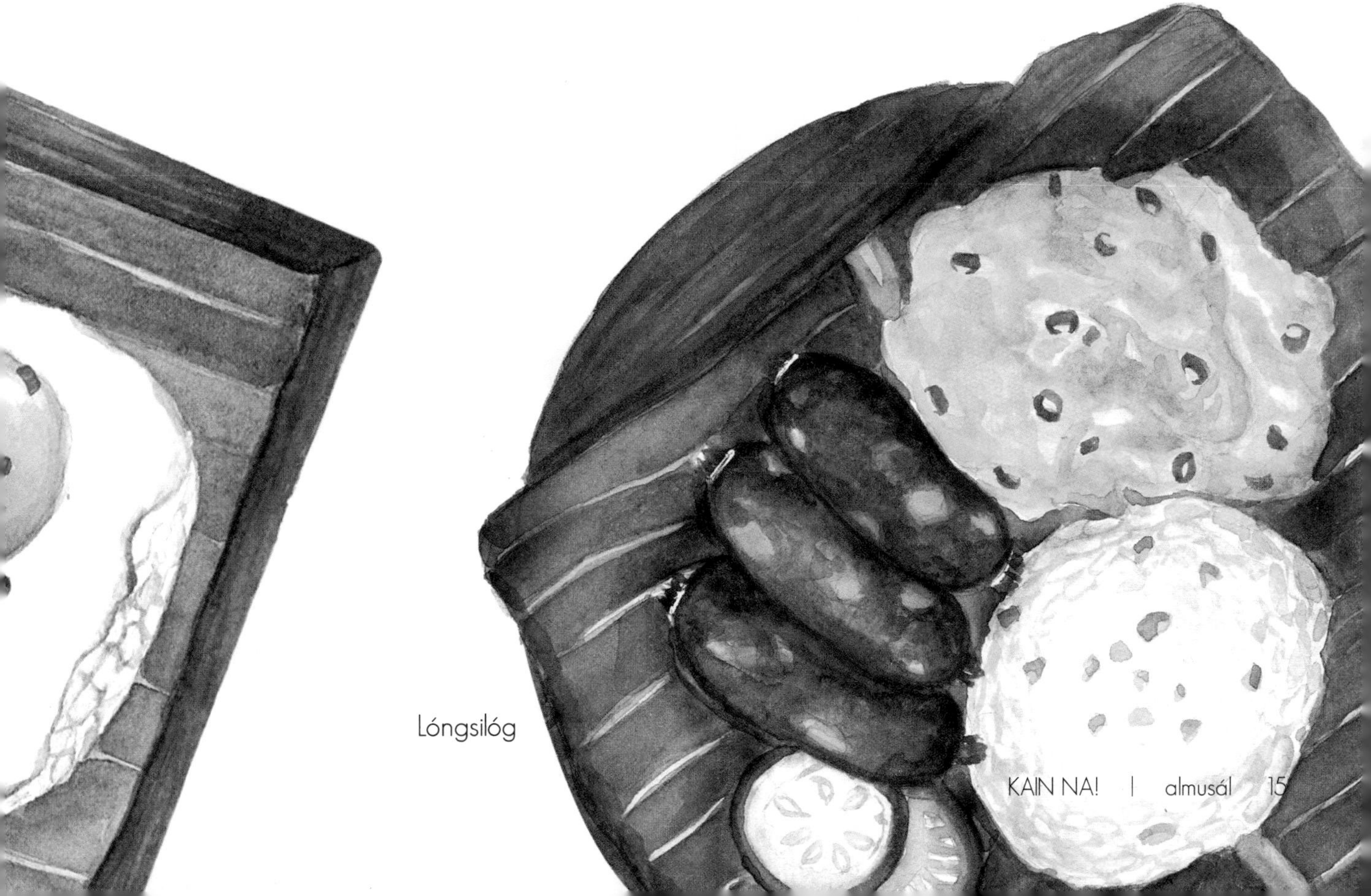

Lóngsilóg

Máginum

/Má·gi·num/

Máginum is the Tausúg morning meal. It can include *bangbáng súg* (rice cakes like *pitís* and *panpán*) partnered with *sattí áyam*, grilled chicken slathered with a sweet, spicy sauce. *Pastél* is rice wrapped with spicy chicken or fish in banana leaf to make a portable meal. Maguindanao *patíl* is cylindrical; the similar Mëranaw *pater* is pyramidical.

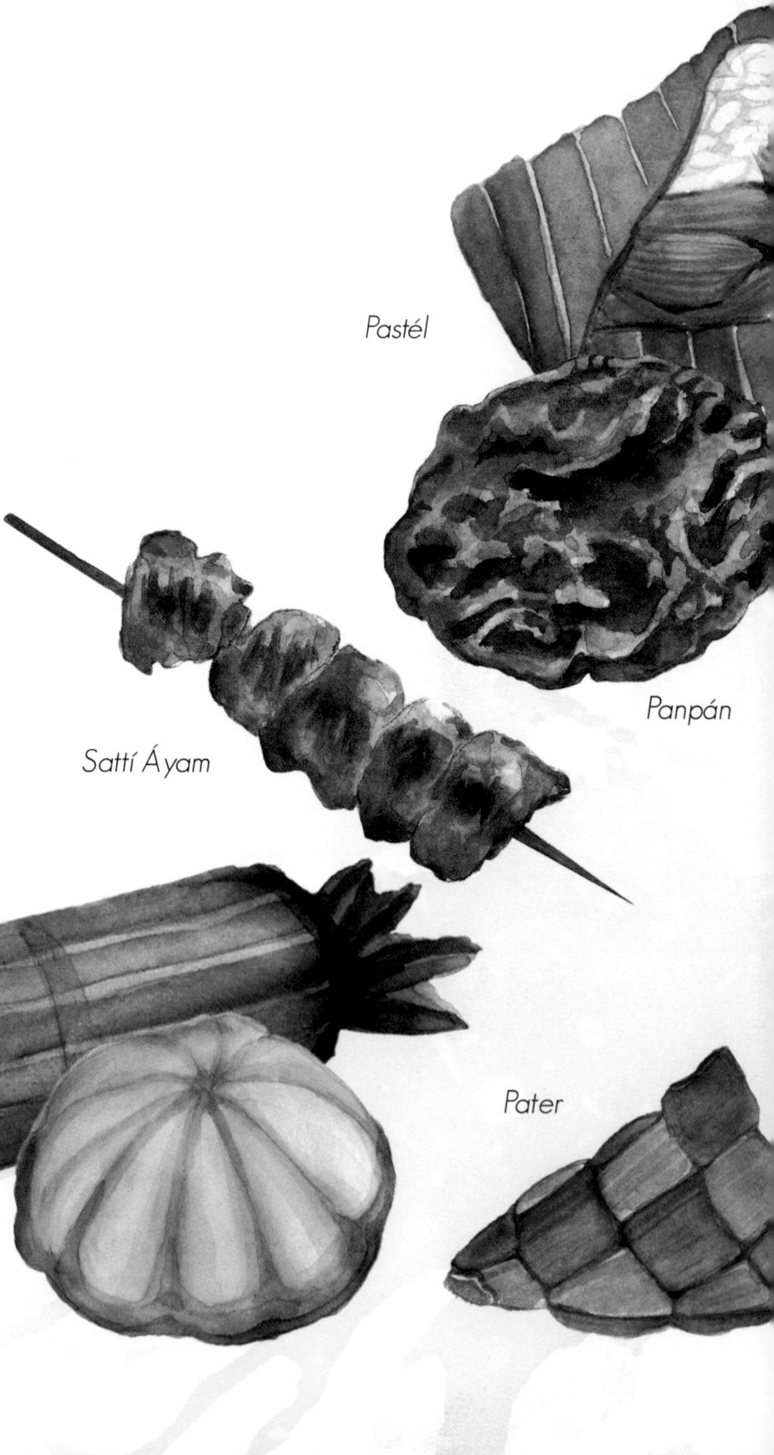

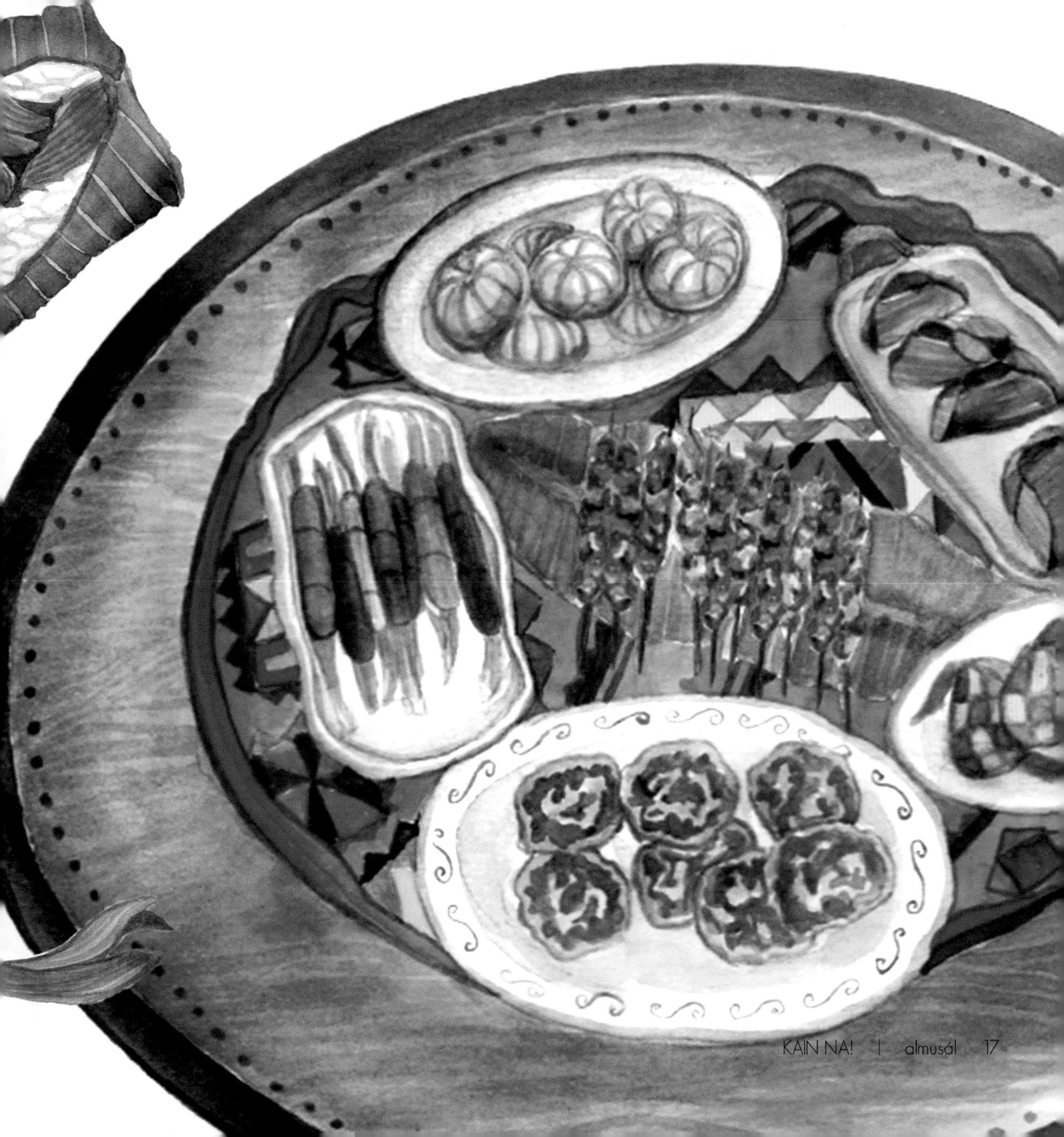

Arróz Cáldo, Góto, at Lúgaw

/A·rróz Cál·do/, /Gó·to/, & /Lú·gaw/

Arróz cáldo (rice [in] broth) loaded with chicken slivers is comfort food. A once cheap alternative is made with beef *góto* (tripe). *Lúgaw*, rice porridge cooked in plain water, is the least costly of the trio sharing Chinese origins. Sold daylong, the dishes can be enriched with toppings of a raw egg, crispy fried bread, and spring onion.

Arróz Cáldo

Lúgaw

Góto

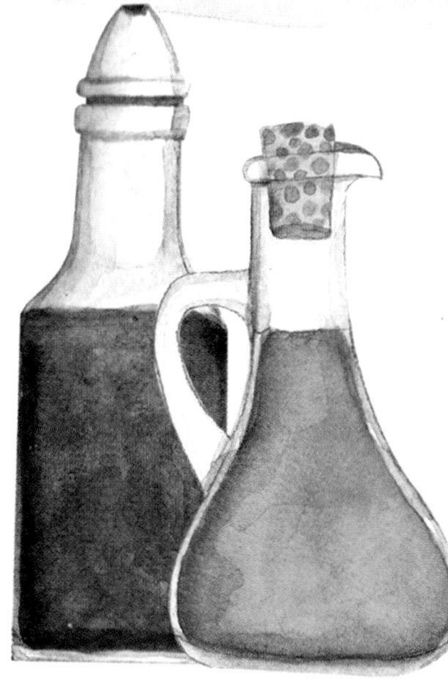

Pansít Batíl Pátong

/Pan·sít Ba·tíl Pá·tong/

Unique to Cagayan Valley is a breakfast dish with *batíl*, a meat sauce of carabeef, carrot, celery, and egg. Just before eating, the *pansít* [noodle] is drenched with *batíl*, thus explaining the last word in the dish's name, pátong: to put something atop. Pansít batíl pátong is commonly served with vinegar and soy sauce.

Míki

/Mí·ki/

A favorite among Ilocanos, *míki* is a soup with freshly made wheat noodles, flavored with chicken broth and shreds of chicken meat, tinted orange with annatto, enriched with smashed *chicharón* (pork crackling), and served with slices of *kutsáy* (garlic chives). A bowl of steaming hot *míki* is particularly favored during *taglamíg*, the local cold season.

Binut-óng

/Bi·nut-óng/

Binut-óng is a banana leaf pouch of glutinous rice and coconut milk boiled in plenty of water. Once the rice absorbs the creamy liquid it transforms into a tender balm reminiscent of oatmeal. It is relished in the morning in Bicol with fried and salted *dáing na isdâ* (fish cut open like a butterfly) and *tsokoláte* (chocolate beverage).

Bátchoy at Púto

/Bát·choy/ & /Pú·to/

Bátchoy is a soup with sliced pork liver, kidney, and small intestines. A touch of *ginamós* (fermented shrimp paste) in the broth flavored by pork bones pushes umami levels up a notch. A shower of crushed *chicharón* (pork crackling) and a splash of vinegar complete the dish. *Púto*, a steamed rice cake, is a favorite companion.

Pinakrô

/Pi·nak·rô/

In the Bicol region's province of Sorsogon, *pinakrô* is prepared by simmering until tender young specimens of the cooking banana called *sabá* in coconut milk with a tiny bit of salt. The cooked bananas may be eaten with a sprinkling of sugar. Bananas, yams, sweet potatoes, and rice offer carbohydrates to the morning meal.

Vinúvuk

/Vi·nú·vuk/

Mornings in the Cagayan Valley Region begin with a porridge made of corn called *mangî* that is processed into cornmeal and then cooked with copious amounts of carabao milk and a little salt. *Vinúvuk* is eaten with sliced spring onion and ground black pepper. Chunks of fried *pindáng na bávi* (local salted pork) are a favored addition.

Júnay

/Jú·nay/

In addition to rice cakes like *pitís* and *panpán,* the Tausug eat *júnay* in the morning. To make the delicacy called *júnay,* banana leaf parcels are filled with raw rice mixed with a little oil, salt, and a paste of *siyúnog láhing* (pounded, coconut roasted till burnt). Coconut has many flavors depending on its handling.

Lútong Báhay

/Lú·tong Bá·hay/

Home Cooking

Even the most original Filipino restaurant, food truck, and *karinderya* (roadside eatery) have their roots in home cooking. The best meals begin with prime ingredients. Fruits are sniffed to test for ripeness, fish eyes are checked to determine freshness, and essential fermented condiments are scrutinized by aroma, texture, color, and taste following traditions. The Philippines is a fine place to learn the secrets of Filipino culinary artisans. Their cooking techniques and sense of savor have been nurtured from grandmother and grandfather to grandchildren over generations. Home cooking brings comfort, unites family members, and strengthens cultural pride. No matter the culinary modes, homes keep alive the traditions they respect most.

Pork Kilawén

Kiníaw na Taníge

Kinílaw. Kilawén. Kilawín

/Ki·ní·law, Ki·la·wén, Ki·la·wín/

Túna, *taníge* (Spanish Mackerel), Cebu *tuyúm* (sea urchin), Iloilo *kaság* (blue crab), Leyte *búkyam* (jellyfish), shrimp, oysters, and other marine delights are fleetingly marinated in spiced vinegar or sour fruit juice, turning them into *kinílaw*, a dish eaten uncooked. *Kilawén* and *kilawín* are meats prepared the same way and served raw. Coconut milk is sometimes added for velvety lusciousness.

Ensaláda

/En·sa·lá·da/

Ensaláda means sálad. While a separate course in western cuisine, *ensaláda* is an accompaniment to other dishes in a Philippine meal. *Ensaládang pakó* features fiddlehead fern; *ensaládang arítos*, the Ilocano "earring sálad," uses *arosép* (miniature grape-shaped seaweed called *lató* in other native languages); *ensaládang rabanós* in southern Mindanao is made with *mooli* radish or daíkon.

Iníhaw

/I·ní·haw/

Roasting, *íhaw*, is done all over the country to fish, seafood, meat, and poultry. In 1521, the world's first circumnavigation crew ate roasted fish served with raw ginger when they reached the Philippines. Some roasts are marinated in artisanal vinegars, sugar, chili, ginger, garlic, annatto, soy sauce, and juices of fruit like *batwán* or *kalamansí*.

Tinóla

/Ti·nó·la/

Tinóla is a soup meal made by boiling chicken, fish, or frog. Variations archipelago-wide are flavored with a selection of ginger, Ilocano *paryá* (bitter gourd), or the leaf of either chili, *kangkóng* (water spinach), *malunggáy* (moringa). Unripe papaya fruit can be added to tenderize meats. Shrimp or fish sauce is served at table for personal salting.

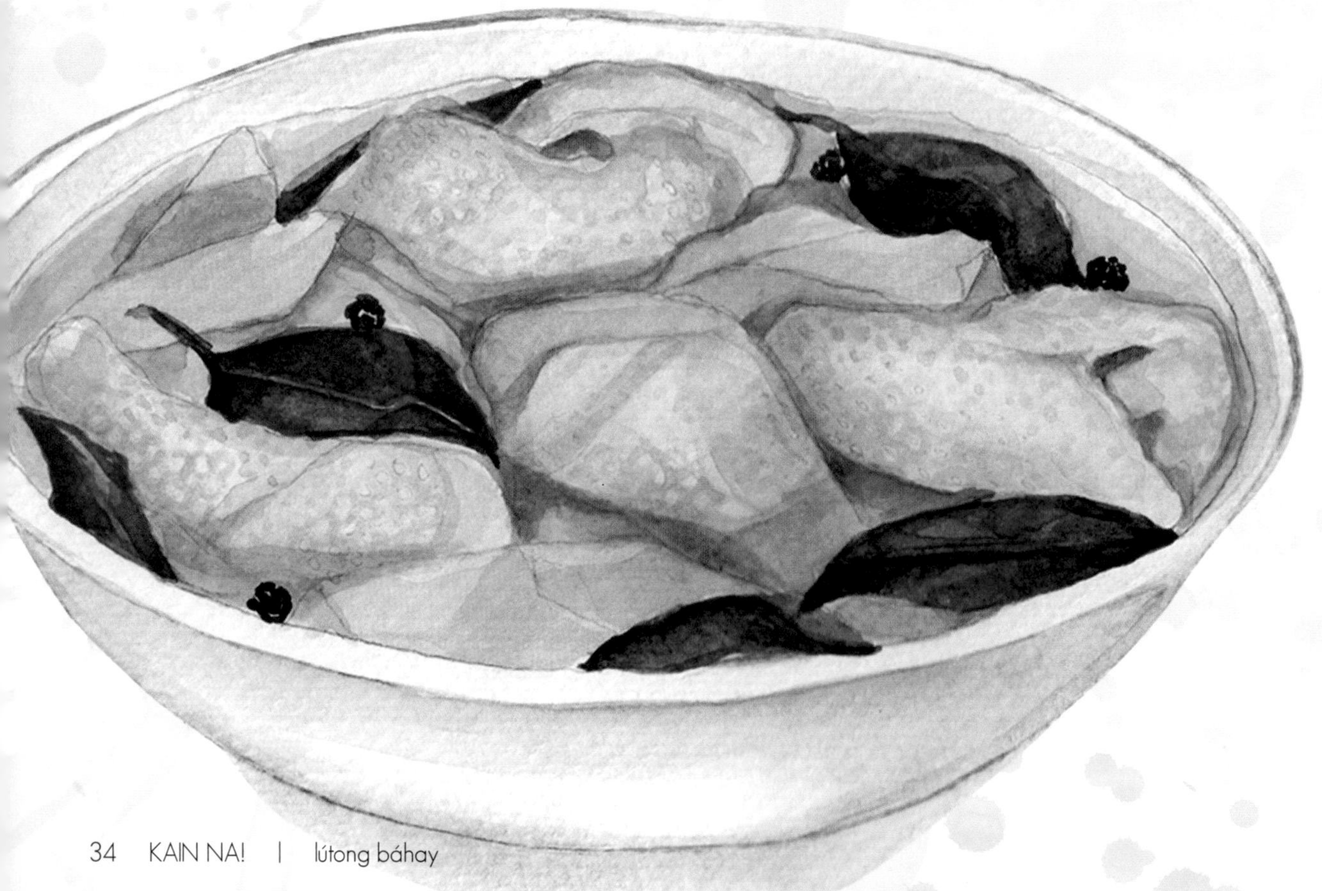

Bulaló

/Bu·la·ló/

Bulaló is a soup named after the Tagalog word for kneecap. In Batangas, Luzon's meat trading capital, only bones with marrow are used. It becomes *nilágang báka* (boiled beef) if meat is added. The dish goes by the names *pakdól* in Leyte where carabao leg is used, as well as *kansí* in Iloilo and Negros Occidental.

Sinigáng

/Si·ni·gáng/

Sourish to mouth-puckering sour is *sinigáng*, a one-pot meal of pork, beef, fish, shrimp, prawn, or in Batanes, flying fish. *Alibangbáng*, *batwán*, guava, *kalamansí*, *kamyás*, mango, *sampálok*, *santól*, or tomato can be the soup's principal souring agent. Rice wash makes the broth cloudy. In the Visayas, it is called *tinóla*; in Cebu, it is *tinówa* or *tówa*.

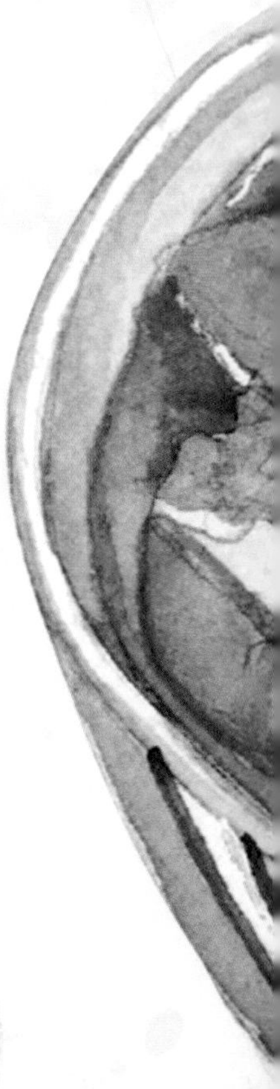

Pork Adóbo

Adóbo

/A·dó·bo/

Hispanic *adóbo*, meaning marinade, transformed into the word for a Philippine dish of meat, poultry, seafood, or vegetables and the way it is cooked. Vinegar is the key ingredient to which annatto, soy sauce, turmeric, bay leaf, black pepper, or coconut milk is added. Every cook takes pride in a personal version of *adóbo* ranging from saucy to dry.

Chicken Adóbo

Pináis

/Pi·ná·is/

Small parcels of shrimp and *búko* (tenderest coconut meat) wrapped with garlic, ginger and salt in banana leaf are simmered in cordial coconut milk. Crab and fish are cooked similarly. Philippine food shows off how to use treasures from the land like the coconut. Native cooks are coconut connoisseurs. *Pináis* is also steamed in a pot of just water.

Piyaparán A Manók

/Pi·ya·pa·rán A Ma·nók/

Mëranaw of Mindanao marinate chicken pieces in coconut milk rich with the well-balanced flavors of turmeric, lemongrass, cinnamon-like cassia leaf, salt, chili, and pungent *palápa* powder. The latter is characterized by charred coconut meat pounded into a family's *palápa* recipe that offers mild to strong pricking of the tongue. All ingredients are stewed to a remarkable finish.

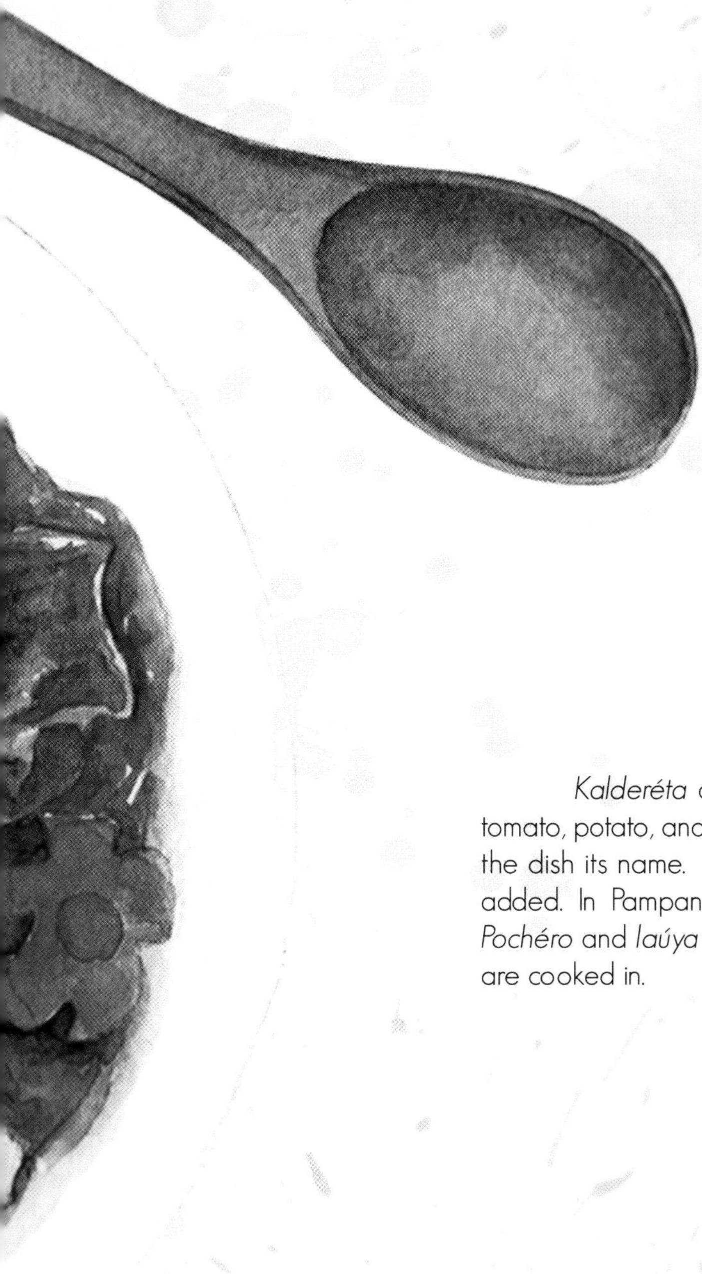

Kalderéta

/Kal·de·ré·ta/

Kalderéta of beef, chicken, or goat is a stew made with tomato, potato, and bell pepper. It was cooked in a *kaldéro*, giving the dish its name. Spanish páprikáa sausage and brined olive are added. In Pampanga, cheese is grated atop it before serving. *Pochéro* and *laúya* are two other dishes named after the pot they are cooked in.

Láing

/Lá·ing/

Láing is a viand of dried and hand-shredded taro leaves and stems that are gently simmered in coconut milk. Chili, shrimp, pork or smoked catfish, ginger, garlic, and bagoong *alamáng* (fermented krill paste) deepen flavors. Bicol is known for its version of *láing*. Taro grew around insular Asia before occidental empires arrived for trade and conquest.

Pinakbët

/Pi·nak·bët/

An assortment of Ilocano vegetables in season is layered in a pot to stew in their juices: ribbed *paryá*, pigeon pea, moringa, *sabidukong* flowers, radish, ókra, young garlic, eggplant, yard-long bean. Flakes of fish or meat, even pieces of *bagnét* (deep-fried pork) or pork *chicharón* (crackling) are added before serving. *Bagoóng monamon* (anchovy paste) is the accompaniment.

Jardinéra

/Har·di·né·ra/

At Lucban and other Quezon towns, a minced pork meat loaf is called *jardinéra* (flower stand or gardener in Spanish). It is rich with ham, sausages, liver spread, cheese. Slices of carrot and red bell pepper are arranged atop the loaf in a floral pattern. Banana leaf lines the *llanéra* (oval metal container) in which the loaf is steamed.

Relyénong Manók

/Rel·yé·nong Ma·nók/

Relyéno means stuffing. Fillings for deboned *manók* (chicken) vary from minced ham, ground pork, Spanish sausage, hard-boiled egg, raisins, miniscule minced carrot, green pea, and green olive. A similar stuffing made with *bangús* (milkfish) meat is used for deboned *bangús*. Chicken *relyéno* is baked or steamed and considered special occasion fare. Milkfish *relyéno* is fried whole.

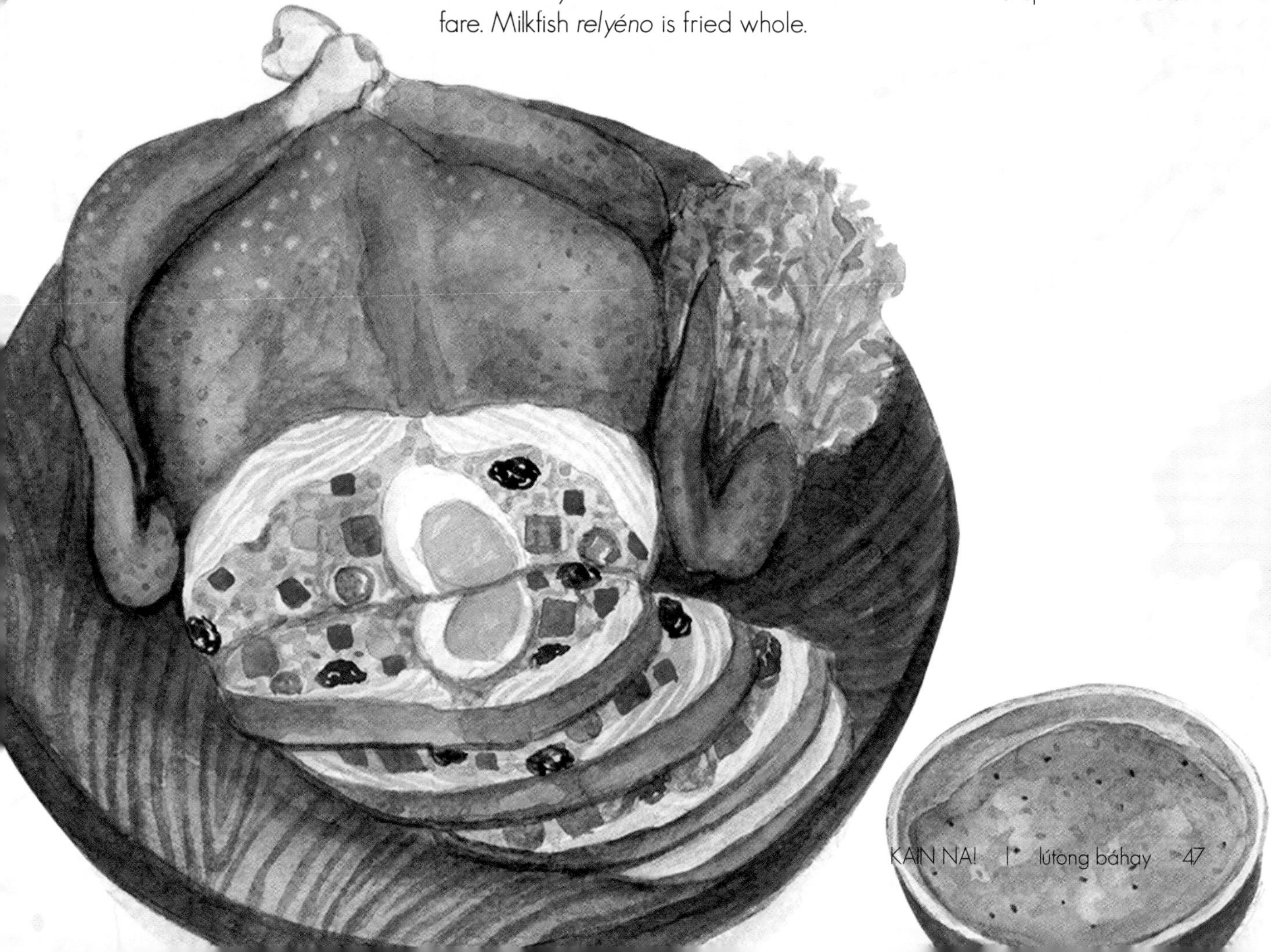

Relyénong Talóng

/Rel·yé·nong Ta·lóng/

Char-grilled *talóng* (eggplant) is stuffed with ground pork, minced potato, carrot, and raisins then covered with beaten egg and fried. Homes and folk food outlets like *túro-túros* also serve the simpler to make *tórtang talóng*, eggplant minus the filling that is dipped in egg and fried. *Túro-túro* means "point-point," because that is how one orders out there.

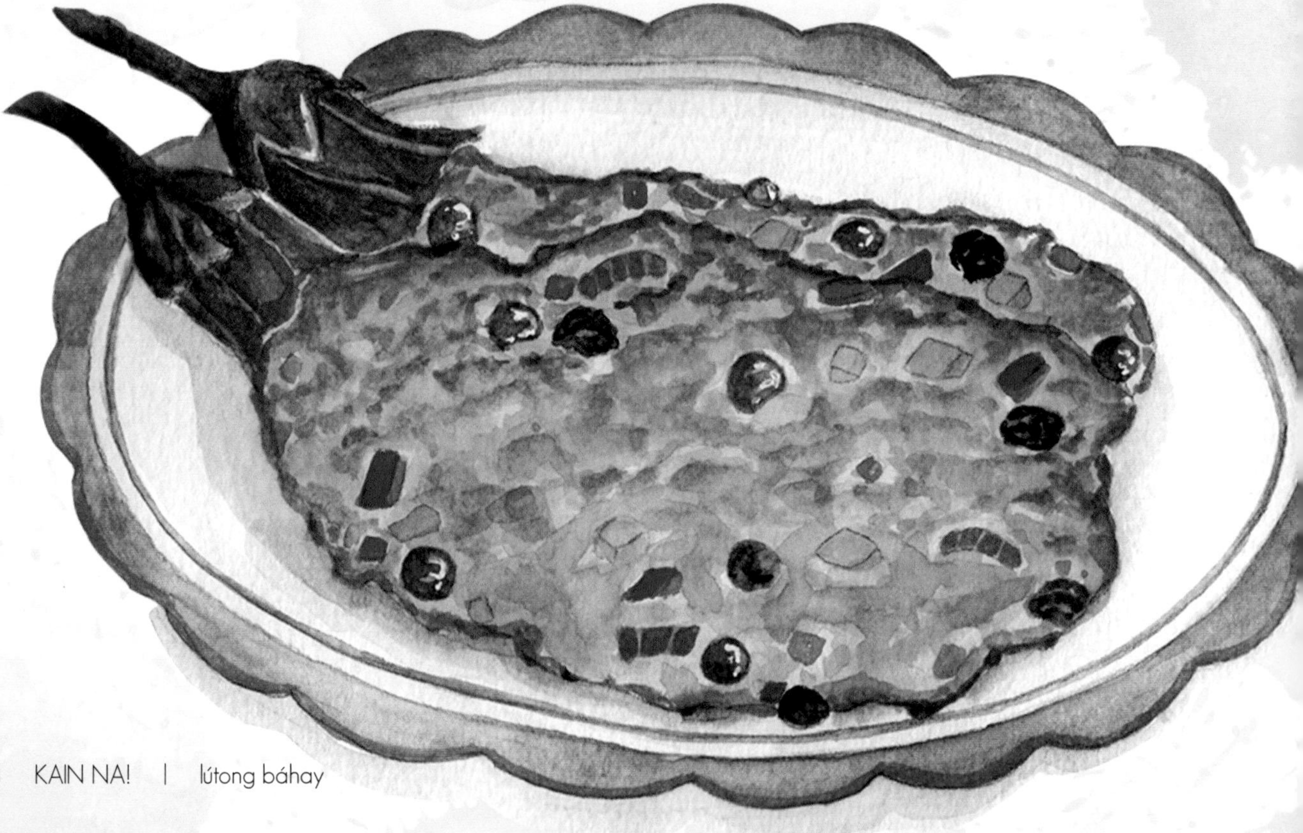

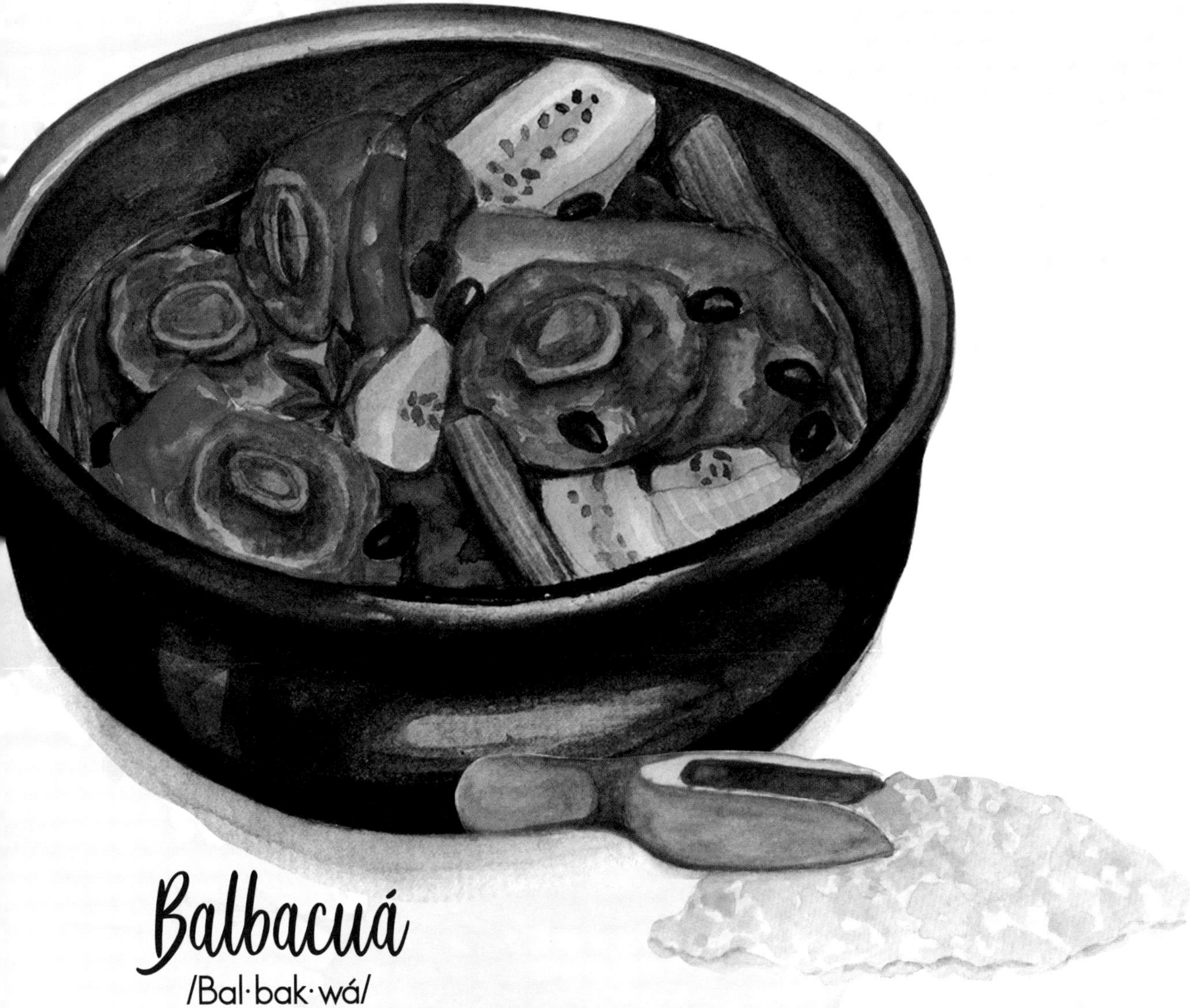

Balbacuá

/Bal·bak·wá/

Hailing from Cebu but spread through many parts of the Visayas, *balbakwá* is a dish of stewed oxtail. It is flavored with annatto, garlic, onions, ginger, star anise, and fermented black beans. Some recipes include ground, roasted peanuts for a slight, unctuous thickening. In Cebu, *balbakwá* is commonly enjoyed with *búgas na maís* (corn grits).

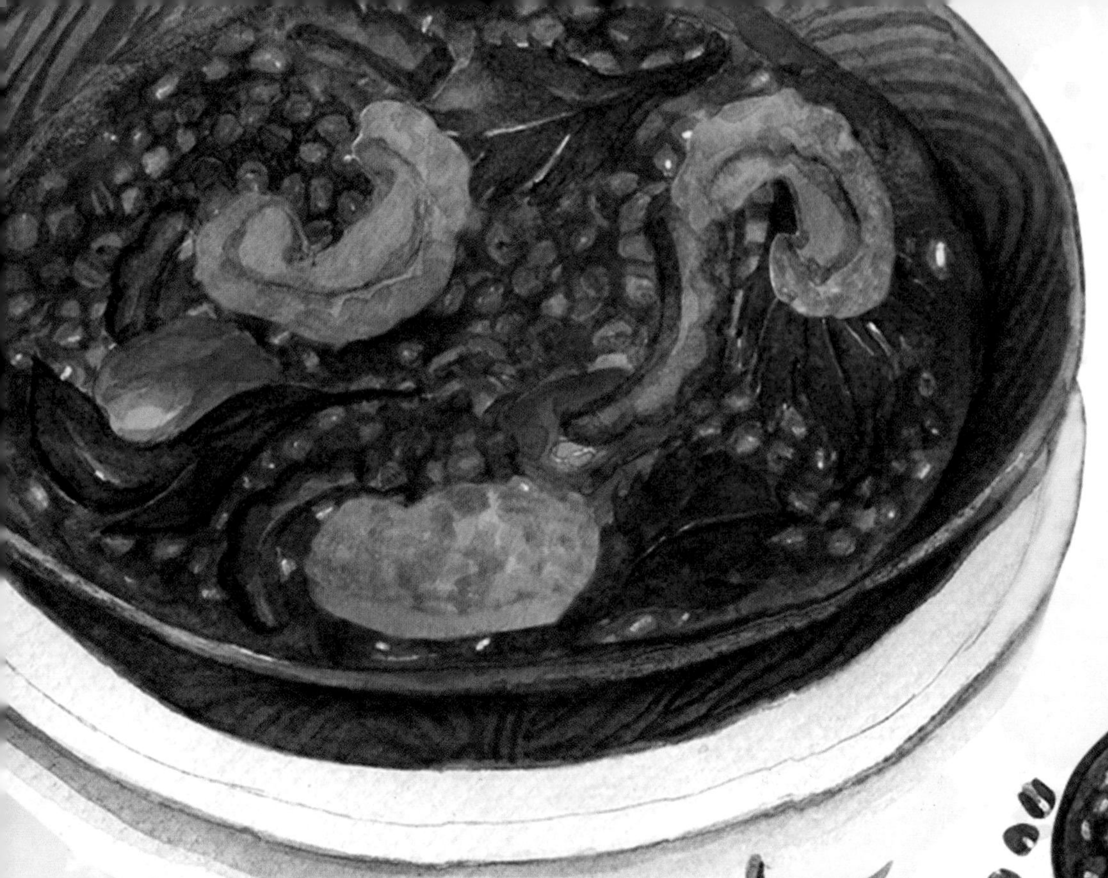

Munggó Guisádo

/Mung·gó Gi·sá·do/

Guisádo is a Spanish cooking technique that Filipinos use widely. It begins with light frying and finishes off with stewing, sometimes for many hours until a sauce is produced. *Munggó* (mung bean), also called *balatóng,* is stewed with tomato or unripe jackfruit and sometimes, coconut milk. Boiled pork, pork crackling, smoked fish, or shrimp can enrich the dish further.

Karé-Karé

/Ka·ré-Ka·ré/

Many hours are needed to make a thick, annatto-tinted stew of tenderest ox tail flavored by ground, toasted rice grain and peanut. Beef shank and honeycombed tripe are often added. *Sítaw* (yard-long bean), tender banana heart, and eggplant complete the dish. *Karé-Karé* is served with *bagoóng* (fish or shrimp paste) that was lightly fried with garlic, onion, and tomato.

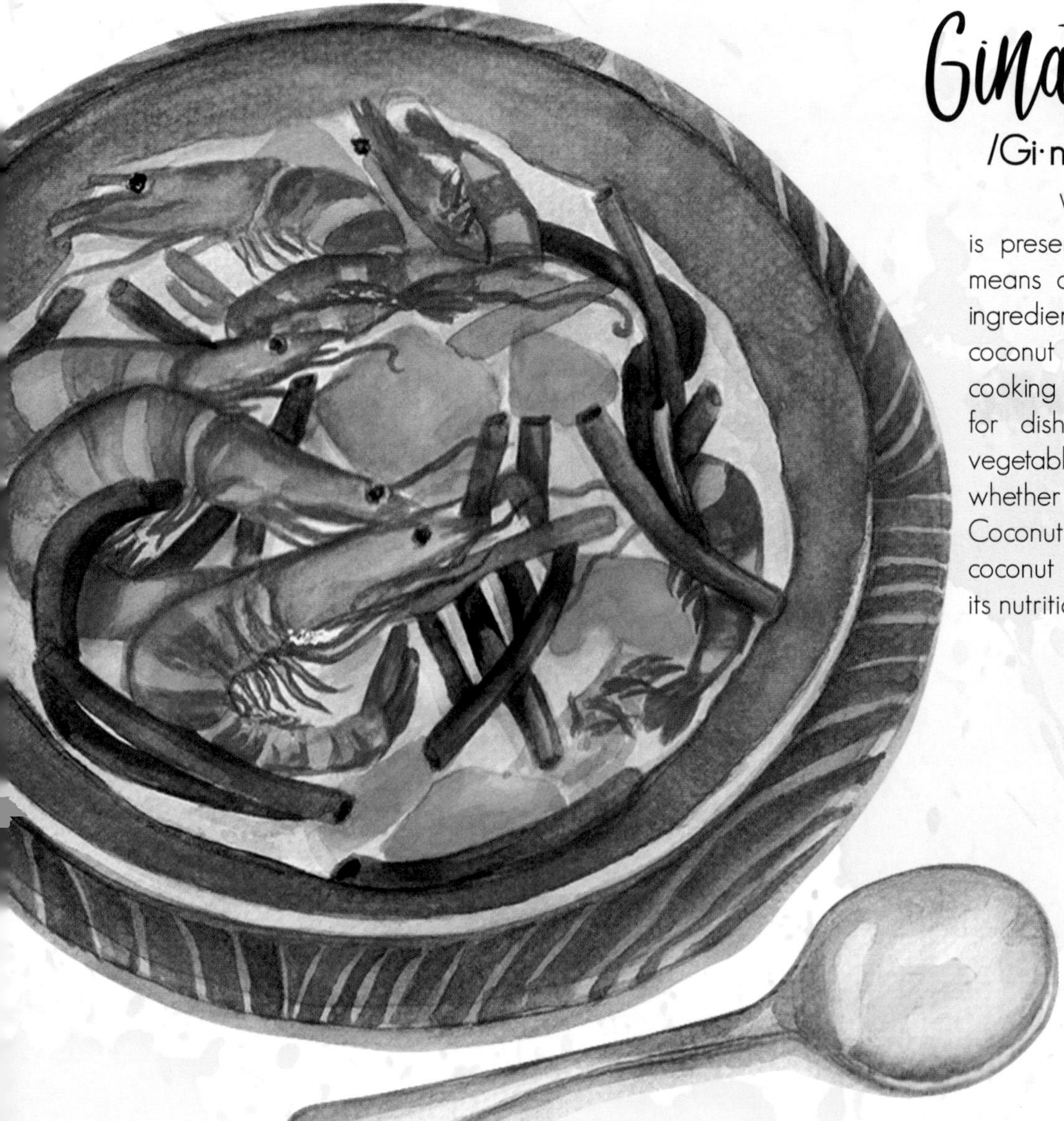

Ginataán

/Gi·na·ta·án/

When the word *ginataán* is present in a food's name, it means coconut milk (*gatá*) is an ingredient. Coconut milk and coconut cream are used as cooking liquids and flavorers for dishes of meats, seafood, vegetables, tubers, and fruits whether they be savory or sweet. Coconut milk is made by grating coconut meat and squeezing out its nutritious liquid.

Tiyúla Itúm

/Ti·yú·la I·túm/

The dish is a Tausug delicacy of boiled beef made fragrant with lemongrass. It employs *súnog láhing*, the burnt coconut paste that makes both the broth and the meat *itúm* or black. In Southern Philippines, the dish is always served at weddings, often also at any other celebrations, and not uncommonly after Ramadan.

Dinengdéng

/Di·neng·déng/

This common Ilocano vegetable braise begins by boiling garlic and shallot in a little water. It is flavored by the essential *bagoóng na isdâ* (fermented fish paste). Slippery *salúyot* (jute), *malunggáy* (moringa), *patóla* (luffa), *labóng* (bamboo shoot), and *munggó* (mung bean) are combined. If sweet potato is added, the *dinengdéng* becomes the dish called *burídibúd.*

Póqui-Póqui

/Pó·ki-pó·ki/

One will never brand scrambled eggs simple after sampling *póqui-póqui* made famous in Ilocos. To a sauté of shallots and tomatoes are added grilled eggplant and beaten egg. Only slim Asian eggplant is proper because it is slightly sweet at its best, likewise the region's salty, fermented fish sauce.

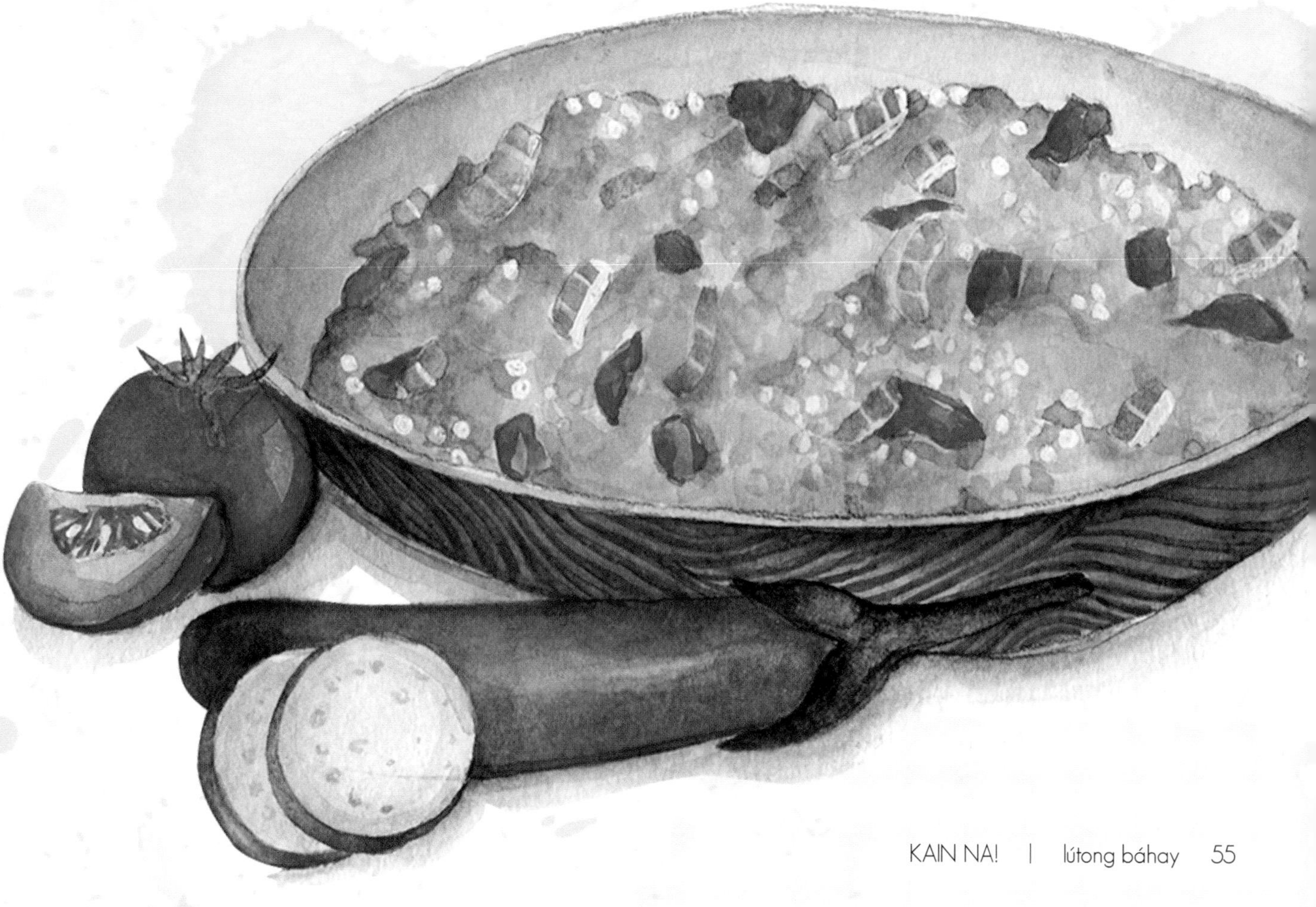

Dinakdákan

/Di·nak·dá·kan/

This is an Ilocano dish of chopped, boiled pig jowls, gently soured with the region's vinegar or *kalamansí* juice and made creamy with crushed, poached pig brain. Some cooks add pork liver. It is almost similar to Pampanga *sísig*. Because pig brain is difficult to obtain, store-bought mayonnaise is often used as a substitute.

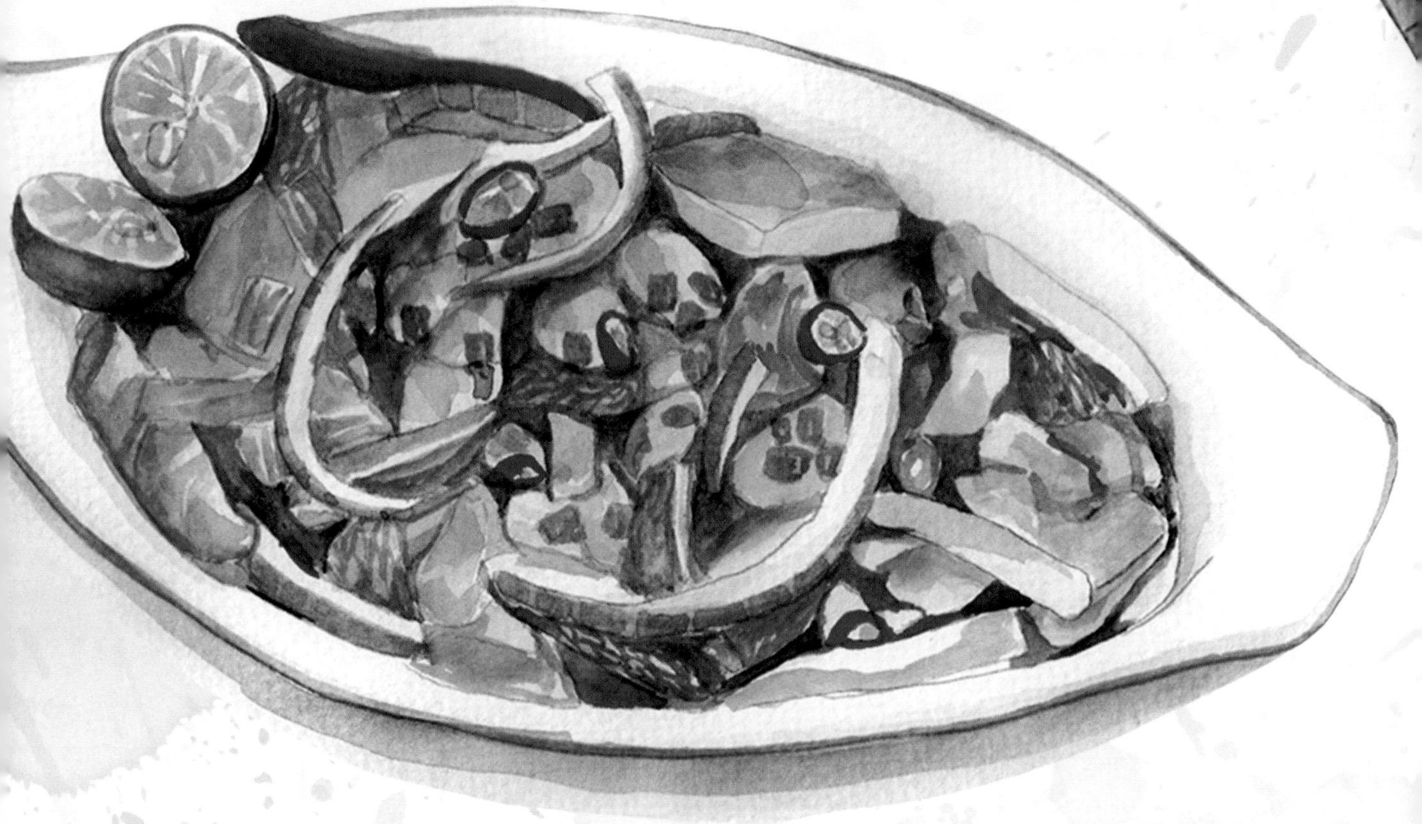

Dinuydúy

/Di·nuy·dúy/

Squash forms the basis for this Ilocano comfort food and many other dishes of the region. *Dinuydúy* is cooked, often to the point of mushiness, with garlic, shallot, fermented krill, and sliced *ampalayá* (bitter gourd). Textural counterpoint comes in the traditional topping: lavish handfuls of pork *chicharón* (crackling). Some versions maintain the *ampalayá* as crisp rather than tender.

Sarciádong Isdâ

/Sar·si·yá·dong Is·dâ/

The Spanish word for sauce, *sálsa,* became *sársa* in many parts of the Philippines. *Sarciádong Isdâ* (fish with sauce) is simple cooking at its finest. The dish must start with the freshest of fish that is first fried. Then it is bathed in tomato sauce into which eggs are lightly scrambled. Home cooks vary versions of the dish.

Humbâ

/Hum·bâ/

The Hookienese term *hóngba* means "red meat." *Humbâ,* a braised pork dish of seeming Chinese origin, is colored by soy sauce regardless of where and how it is interpreted around the Philippines. Dried banana blossoms are used in Batangas and Mindoro; fermented soybean and *tajúre* (fermented soybean cake) in the Visayas; and *tabléya* (kakáw cakes) in Leyte.

Binagoóngang Báboy

/Bi·na·go·ó·ngang Bá·boy/

Any dish described as *binagoóngan* means it is seasoned with *bagoóng* (fermented fish or shrimp paste). *Báboy* is a native word for pork. For this viand, pork cubes are sautéed in onion, garlic, and tomato before *bagoóng* is added. Water is then added, and the ingredients allowed to simmer till the pork softens and all the flavors blend harmoniously.

Lechón Kawali

/Le·chón Ka·wa·lì/

Lechón means pig in Spanish, and usually conjures up images of the spit-roasted whole pig served at a fiesta. *Kawalì* is a traditional frying pan. To make this dish, pork *liyémpo* (belly) is fried till crisp. It is served with the sweetish liver sauce used for the fiesta *lechón* or, simply, soy sauce tempered by citrus juice.

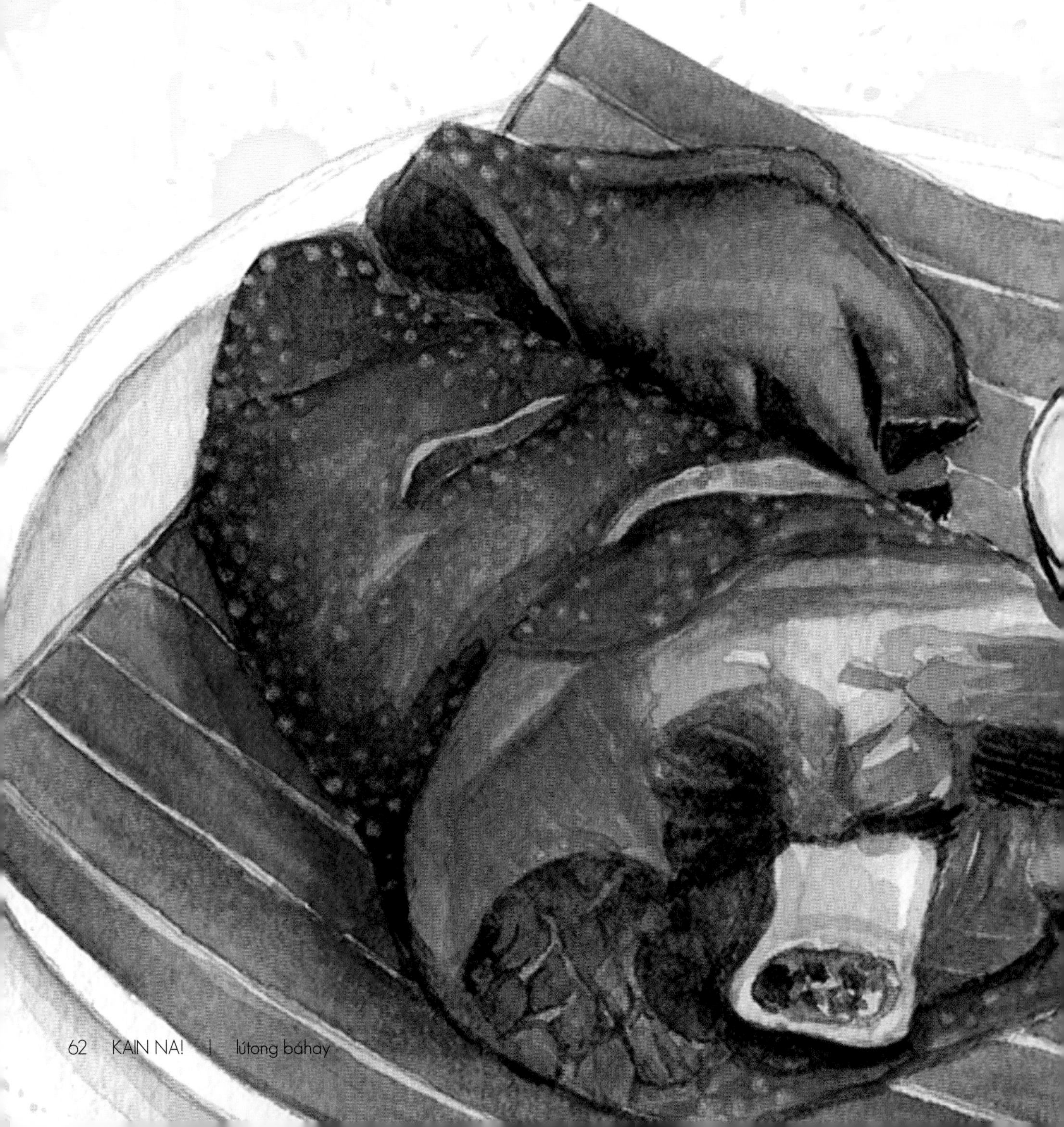

Crispy Páta

/Crispy Pá·ta/

Thrice-fried pork knuckles are served with papaya pickles and a dipping sauce of vinegar or soy sauce and *kalamansí* juice. The more bubbles or blisters in the fried skin, the better. Frying also makes *lechón kawáli* (deep-fried pork belly) that can become *binagoóngan* with the addition of cooked *bagoóng* [fermented krill or fish paste].

Laúya

/La·ú·ya/

Throughout northern and central Philippines, *laúya* is a stew usually made with pork knuckles, although beef versions exist. Vegetables bulk up the dish to which a touch of sourness must be added. In Iloilo unripe jackfruit or *batwán* fruit pulp is the souring agent. In Ilocos, local artisanal vinegars season the stew's potatoes and cabbage.

Éstofádo

/És·to·fá·do/

While *éstofádo* is generic in Spanish for stew, it means two dishes in Filipino. One is a sweetish, soy-colored stew of duck or pork knuckle and cooked banana, perfumed with bay leaf and garlic. The second *éstofádo* is close to the Hispanic template with wine and butter or a tomato sauce used for ox tongue.

Meryénda

/Mer·yén·da/

An Afternoon Snack

Meryénda is a must in the Philippines. Some of the most interesting, provincially diverse, and delicious foods are served as *pantawíd gútom*, meaning "to bridge the hunger gap" between lunch and dinner. One can survive eating just *merienda* fare. The menu is as simple as a boiled yam, a satisfying noodle soup or stir-fry, a small sandwich, or a steamed *siopao* bun. Elegant tables are heavy with trays of *ensaymáda* (coiled bread saturated in butter and topped with edam cheese), *tórta* (sponge cakes), and pies. Peddlers sell a diversity of *kakanín* (rice cakes and rice puddings). *Merienda cena* combines a few heavy foods associated with *cena* (dinner).

Pansít Palábok

/Pan·sít Pa·lá·bok/

Only in the Philippines does *pansít* mean noodle. It derives from a Hokkien term for "ready-made food" revealing migrations of southern Chinese to the Philippines since the 16th century. True to its adjective *palábok* (embellishment), this *bíhon* (rice noodle) dish is topped with a flavorful annatto sauce decorated with shrimp, squid, smoked fish, *wansúy* (coriander) leaves, and fried garlic.

Pansít Cantón

/Pan·sít Can·tón/

It is legendary that Cantonese cooks introduced this popular stir-fry of wheat noodles. It has a thick sauce, shrimp, pork, chicken, carrot, cabbage, and other vegetables in season. *Pansít cantón* is often served at birthdays during which noodles are to be eaten without cutting them. It is believed that the longer the noodles, the longer the celebrant's life.

Pansít Mámi

/Pan·sít Má·mi/

This is a flavorful soup of fine egg noodles and shredded chicken or beef. A shower of finely sliced spring onions and crisp-fried garlic confetti complete it. Ma Mon Lok sold *mi* (noodles) and earned enough to buy the building at the corner where he began as a peddler. *Mámi* means Ma's noodles; in Hokkienese, "meat with noodles."

Pansít Chóco En Su Tínta

/Pan·sít Chó·co En Su Tín·ta/

The black ink (*tínta*) of squid (*chóco* and *pusít*) is a thickener. Mixed into *sótanghón* (rice vermicelli), it becomes an enricher for a beloved noodle snack. Toasted garlic, thin slices of sour *kamyás* fruit, and Chinese celery top the dish, also called *pansít pusít*. It became popular in Cavite City where the Spanish galleon port was.

Pansít Habháb

/Pan·sít Hab·háb/

Sariyaya and Lucban towns in Quezon Province seem to be where *pansít habháb* began. *Habháb* is best translated as "to gobble up" food. Brown *míki* (wheat noodles), soy sauce, fresh onion rings, and sugarcane vinegar characterize the dish available at marketplaces. The stir-fry is eaten directly off a square piece of banana leaf on which it is served.

Ensaymáda

/En·say·má·da/

The queen of Philippine breads is *ensaymáda*. It is fancier and lighter than its Spanish prototype. Today's interpretation has an exuberance of butter. An exaggeration of grated Edam cheese and sugar are toppings; salted duck egg is an alternative. Chinese ham, *úbe* jam, native cheese, and even a hint of chili can be folded in.

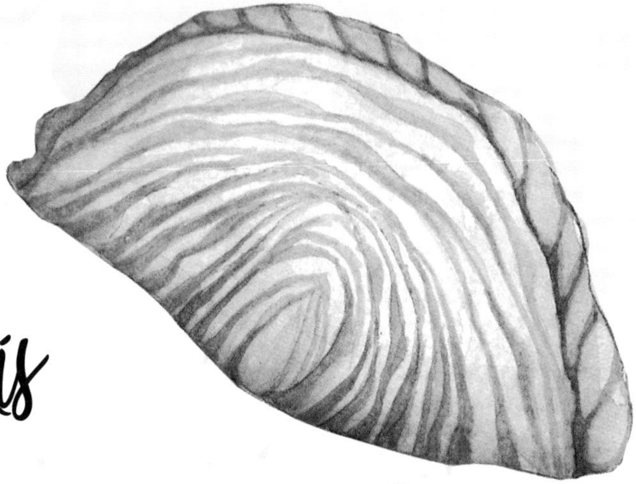

Empanáda Kaliskís

/Ém·pa·ná·da Ka·lis·kís/

Empanáda means a "meat pie"; *kaliskís*, (fish scales). The terms poetically describe the fried article, an effect produced by the intricate marrying and layering of two kinds of dough, one made with oil, the other with water. The filling tends to be one of diced chicken, hard-boiled egg, carrot, and potatoes bound in a creamy, mildly peppery sauce.

Vígan Empanáda

/Ví·gan Ém·pa·ná·da/

Inside a crisp, rice-flour wrapper tinged golden orange from annatto is a pillow of unripe papáya, mung bean, egg, and the locally conjured pork sausage. One's first bite opens a cavity into which sugarcane vinegar should be spooned. Thankfully the beloved turnover is easily found and no longer sold only at Vígan's church plaza in the afternoons.

Lumpiyáng Úbod

/Lum·pi·yáng Ú·bod/

Lumpia is the Philippine spring roll, named after a Hokkien term for the ultra-thin wrapper made with rice flour or beaten egg. Affluent families in Bacolod and Iloilo feast on a version filled with *úbod*, heart of coconut palm. *Lumpiyáng úbod* at its finest is a symphony of textural tenderness harmonized with the understated, natural sweetness of *úbod*.

Dinuguán

/Di·nu·gu·án/

Nothing is wasted in the native kitchen, not even meat blood (*dugô*). *Dinuguán* is a sourish soup, ranging from thin to thick, made with blood and meat from chicken, beef, carabeef, or pork. Versions dot the archipelago. In Ilocos, it is called *dinardaráan*. Bulacan's *serkéle* features beef innards. A steamed white rice cake often accompanies the dish.

Tamáles

/Ta·má·les/

Mexican corn *tamal* inspired a Filipino version generally made of rice flour, coconut milk, annatto-colored water, chicken, pork, shrimp, and peanut. Wrapped in banana leaf, *tamáles* are steamed or boiled. Spanish sausage and Chinese ham may be included. Samar *tamálos* contains pork *húmba*. A fiery mix of bean-thread noodle and chicken hides inside every benign-looking Zamboanga *tamale*.

Ginataáng Halò-Halò

/Gi·na·ta·áng Ha·lò-Ha·lò/

Ginataán means "cooked with coconut milk"; *halò-halò* means "mix-mix". Together, they represent a sweet, creamy soup with different sweet potatoes and yams, tapioca, balls of rice or *burí* palm flour, as well as slices of cooked banana and ripe jackfruit. *Úbe* yam turns it lavender. Look for it as *paridosdós* in Ilocos and *binignít* in Cebu.

Bibíngka

/Bi·bíng·ka/

Bibíngka is a rice cake traditionally cooked with two fires: one from the stove on which batter in its clay pan sits; the other from burning charcoal on a lid. Carabao milk cheese, salted duck egg, and grated coconut meat are embellishments. *Bibíngkang galapóng* uses rice flour and *bibíngkang malagkít*, (sticky rice). Grated cassava is also made into *bibíngka*.

Lútong Kalsáda

/Lú·tong Kal·sá·da/

Street Food

At crossroads and piers, parking lots and bus terminals, churchyards and town plazas, near schools and hospitals, along well-trodden lanes in citified neighborhoods and beach barrios alike the nose is first assaulted, but then lured by the strong aromas of street cooking. Street food is cooked fresh, upon request, and on the spot. Selections are quick to prepare and easy to eat. Highly affordable, they frequently use cheap ingredients and beckoning spicy dips. Find folk food on tables brought out from the house mornings and afternoons when pedestrian traffic is high. Watch out for push-carts that pop up wherever business can be brisk.

VOTE
VOTE
MAYNI
mar
24
ICECREAM

Turón at Banána-Cué

/Tu·rón/ & /Ba·ná·na-kyú/

Sabá is the chubby, native cooking banana. A *sabá* rolled up in a rice-flour wrapper, deep-fried, and served gleaming with droplets of candied sugar is called *turón*. It traces to Spanish *turrón*, luscious nougats, and not *turón*, the field mouse. A banana-cue is a syrup-coated *sabá* on a barbeque stick. Both are best eaten immediately after deep-frying.

Chicharón

/Chi·cha·rón/

Chicharón is pork crackling crisped in its own lard. Varieties use different parts: *balát*, pork rind; "cocktail," skin without fat; *lamán*, some meat still attached to sweetbreads; *éspesyál lamán*, loin; *bitúka*, pig or cow intestines. Chicken skin is also made into *chicharón*. Pork's frilly mesentery becomes *chicharón bulaklák*, indeed similar to a *bulaklák*, meaning "flower."

Ókoy

/Ó·koy/

"The thinner, the crisper, the better," say fastidious fans of *ókoy*, a circular fritter made with rice flour, although corn and wheat flour offer variations. Shrimp so tiny their eyes resemble periods star in one version. Sweet potato, unripe papaya, bean sprout, and spring onion can be added. Enjoy *ókoy* with a chili and raw garlic spiked vinegar dip.

Barbecué

/Bar·bi·kyú/

BBQ means barbeque in street lingo. Pork BBQ is small, thin meat slices threaded on a bamboo skewer. *Ísaw báboy* is pork intestine solely. All pork parts are marinated in banana ketchup, *kalamansí juice*, and soy sauce before grilling till slightly charred. It comes with a dip of vinegar piquant from raw red onion and chili.

Chicken *atáy* (liver), *batikúlon* (gizzard), and *púso* (heart) are similarly flavored. Philippine Airlines or PAL BBQ means wings. On skewers, too, are fish or squid balls for frying on demand and dousing with soy and sweet-spicy sauces.

Kwék-Kwék at Toknéneng

/Kwék-Kwék/ & /Tok·né·neng/

A poultry sound roots the moniker *kwék-kwék* for fried quail eggs in annatto-orange batter. Chicken and duck eggs prepared similarly are called *toknéneng*. The partner for all three is a dip of soy sauce and *kalamansí* juice or *pinakurát* vinegar. Street food is affordable, portable, and perfect with a cool drink.

Balút

/Ba·lút/

A 16- to 21-day-old embryo is inside *balút*, a boiled duck egg. *Balút pénoy* is all yolk: *masabáw*, if soupy; *tuyô*, if dry. Crack the eggshell open, and sprinkle sea salt inside as one eats the contents. *Prítong balút* is a fried *balút* coated with batter. A deep-fried, day-old chick is sold as Super Chick or Day-O.

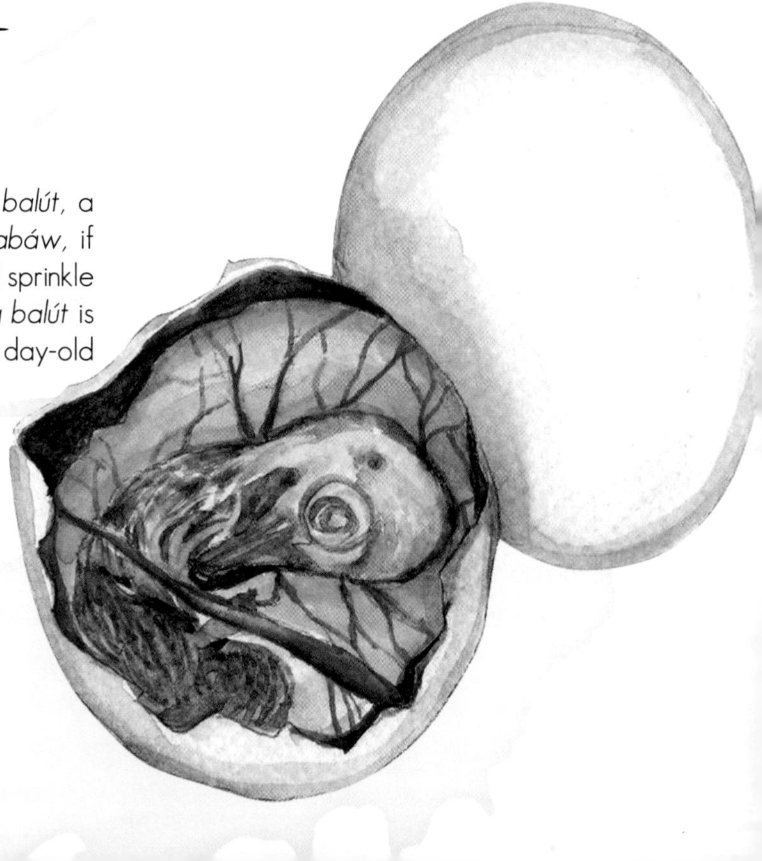

Nilágang Maís at Nilágang Ságing

/Ni·lá·gang Ma·ís/ & /Ni·lá·gang Sá·ging/

Lága (to boil) is a simple cooking process. *Maís* (corn) boiled in its husk and *ságing* (banana, usually the cooking *sabá* variety) or *kamóte* (sweet potato) in their skins, as well as *manî* (peanut) in its shell are highly common snacks and easy, inexpensive foods to allay hunger. *Maís* and *kamóte* are also sold roasted.

SPECIAL
ICE CREAM
Manila
ICE CREAM
94

Sorbétes

/Sor·bé·tes/

Colorfully painted carts sell home-style *sorbétes* (sherbet, but also meaning ice cream with little milk). Among popular flavors are *buko* (coconut), chocolate, corn, *queso* (cheese), avocado, *úbe* (purple yam), *langkâ* (jackfruit). They are scooped into an *ápa* (cone) or a bread bun. "Dirty Ice Cream," a nickname for street sherbet, is loaded with affection, even as it cautions.

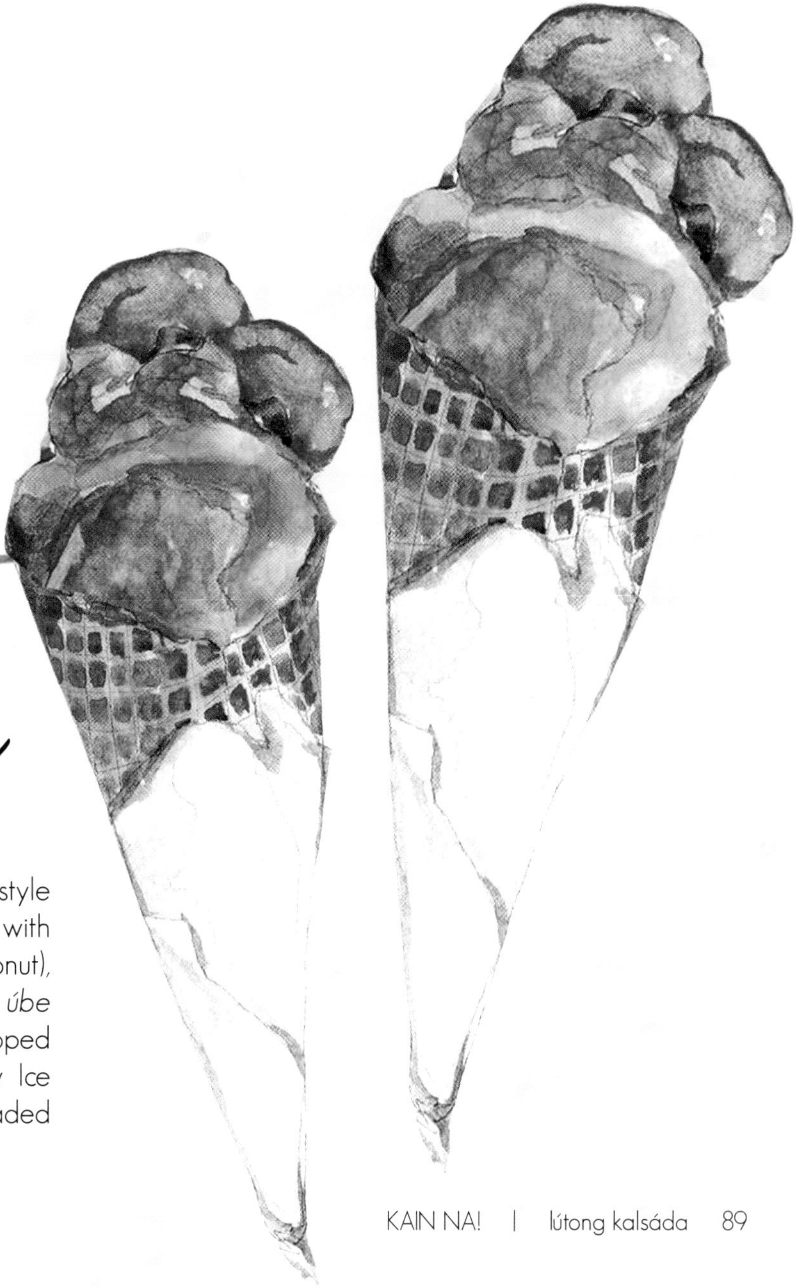

Binatóg

/Bi·na·tóg/

Dried corn kernels puffed up by soaking in saltwater are boiled till very soft to become *binatóg*. The snack is especially delicious mixed with grated *lukarón* ("teenage" coconut), a little salt and sugar, and a good glug of coconut, carabao, or evaporated milk. *Binatóg* vendors announce their presence by rhythmically striking a cowbell.

Prútas at Singkamás

/Prú·tas/ & /Sing·ka·más/

Prútas (fruits) like ripe pineapple, mango, and papáya are sold peeled, sliced, and ready to eat. "Green mango" means unripe, sour mango. It becomes a gourmand treat as a green mango sandwich: fruit cheeks with a filling of umami-rich *bagoóng* (shrimp or fish paste) between them. On a hot day, *singkamás* (jicama turnip) is sweetish and thirst quenching.

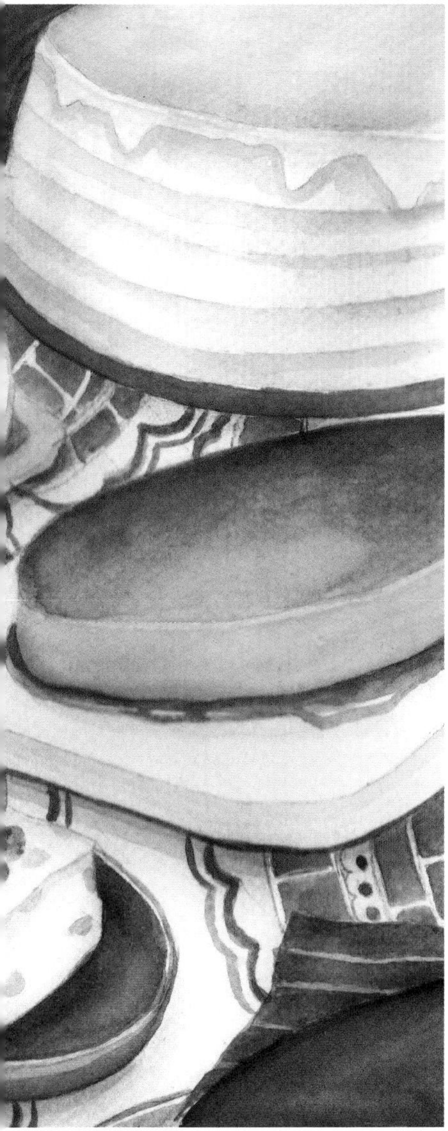

Panghimágas

/Pang·hi·má·gas/

Desserts

Himágas is an old Tagalog word meaning to eat sweets at the end of a meal. It implies that the favored flavor to have lingering after a Philippine meal should be sweetish to saccharine. Wild honeys, sugar cakes from palms, fresh juice straight from biting into a length of sugarcane, and ripe tropical fruits were the earliest *panghimágas*. They were incorporated into complex desserts like ice creams, sherbets, cakes, puddings, pies, fancy meringues, and candies as cooking techniques and culinary equipment expanded. Giving desserts flair, fancy, and flavor is very competitive whether at food floors in malls or top-tier establishments.

Mínatamís

/Mí·na·ta·mís/

Fruits from the backyard and the farm like *sabá* banana, breadfruit, guava, and mango were turned into *mínatamís* (meaning sweetened) packed in sugarcane syrup. Tiny *dáyap* (lime) and *santól* (cotton fruit) were even incised with florid patterns. When syrupy fruits were dried, they became jewel-like candies for fiestas once called *abrillantadas* because they sparkled brilliantly.

Panutsá at Turón

/Pa·nut·sá/ & /Tu·rón/

Sugarcane sugarcakes are called *panutsá*. They come plain or studded with peanuts or coconut rashers in many provinces. Nipa palm syrup solidifies into thin *pakaskás* cakes to nibble on. *Píli*, an endemic nut, and cashew, introduced from the New World, have been made into Spanish *mazapán* (marzipan) and *turrón* (nougat) in which insular Asian *dáyap* (lime) substitutes for lemon.

Pastíllas de Leche

/Pas·tíl·yas de Le·che/

Finest white sugar is cooked ever so slowly into milk (*leche*) from carabao over low heat to make the splendid Filipino nougat (*pastíllas de leche*). The person cooking must be patient and watchful. The slightest scorching destroys a batch. One can purchase *pastíllas de leche* by the bottleful to eat by the spoonful, or as individually wrapped bite-sized pieces.

Pastíllas de Frútas

/Pas·tíl·yas de Frú·tas/

Plumping the meat of tamarind, red tomato, jackfruit, *santól*, pineapple, and mango in syrup until all the liquid has been absorbed makes *pastíllas de frútas* (fruit nougats). For fiestas, each hand-rolled, bite-sized gem is packaged in a paper *pabalát* (wrapper) with an elaborate hand-cut tassel called *bórlas de pastíllas* that can feature a rural scene or a guest's name.

Úbe Halayá

/Ú·be Ha·la·yá/

In the Philippines, *halayá* means jam used as a spread for bread and a luscious, pudding-like dessert. *Úbe* (purple yam) from Bohol, where it is called *kinampáy*, is celebrated for its deep purple color, large size, and refined texture when cooked. To make *halayá*, boiled *úbe* is mashed, sugar slowly added, and both butter and condensed milk folded in.

Búko Pandán

/Bú·ko Pan·dán/

The softest coconut flesh comes from the young nut called *búko*. It is scraped into strands and combined with cubes of *ágar-ágar* (seaweed gelatin) turned green by juice of *pandán* (fragrant screwpine). All-purpose dairy cream or coconut cream and white sugar complete the chilled dessert, sometimes listed as a sálad. Tiny fruit of *káong* (sugar palm) can be included.

Mája Blánca

/Má·ja Blán·ca/ or /Má·ha bláng·ka/

The anise-kissed pudding of rice flour, coconut or cow milk, and sugar is likened to a fair (*blancá*), young woman (*mája*). Every serving is topped by curd-like *latík* made by reducing coconut milk until its oil is extracted. *Mája blánca maíz* is a variation that uses grated young corn passed through coarse muslin to assure finest texture.

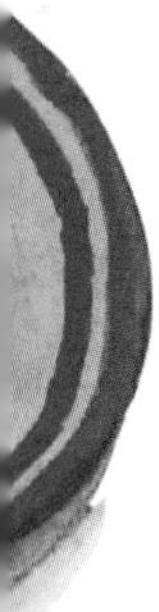

Leche Flán

/Le·che Flán/

Philippine *leche flán* (milk flan) is sweeter and more egg-rich than its Hispanic prototype called *flán de leche* that is made with cow milk. Native versions use carabao milk and even combinations of condensed and evaporated milks. *Dáyap* (lime) rind offers a subtle fragrance while balancing the dessert's fabled luxurious savor. It is the traditional star among fiesta desserts.

Sans Rivál

/Sans Ri·vál/ or /Sans Ri·bál/

Before World War II, this baked masterpiece had multiple, thinnest layers of hardened merengue, sweet butter, and fine almond slivers. Over time cashew became the favored nut. Miniature versions, especially those from Pampanga, are much desired. *Sans rivál* is French for "without rival." Spanish patisserie and American home economics for public school are part of Philippine dessert traditions.

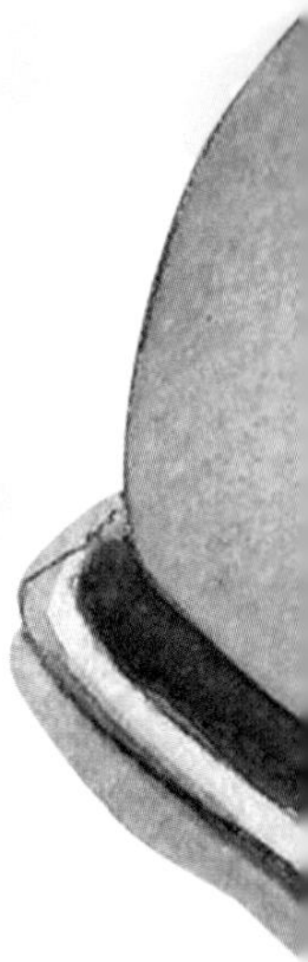

Brázo de Mercédes

/Brá·zo de Mer·cé·des/

The identity of Mercedes remains a mystery. But the white merengue roll does resemble a *brázo* (arm). The dessert has become so popular one can purchase it in many bakeshops. At its finest, *brázo de Mercédes* is a romance of egg whites turned into light fragility partnered with a silken, golden, egg-rich, vanilla custard.

Pulútan

/Pu·lú·tan/

Bar Chow

Local customs archipelago-wide promote drinking with a companion and eating casual fare that can be picked up (*púlot*) with the fingers. *Pulútan* is meant to be shared and can come in group-size portions. Fancy drinking foods need a spoon or a fork. Many families have menfolk who pride themselves in preparing food appropriate for drinking sessions. Chow is often salty to increase the craving for beverages and to cause one to sweat out body heat from alcohol. Much of the *pulútan* menu is fat-rich supposedly to line the stomach and prepare it to cope during drinking bouts.

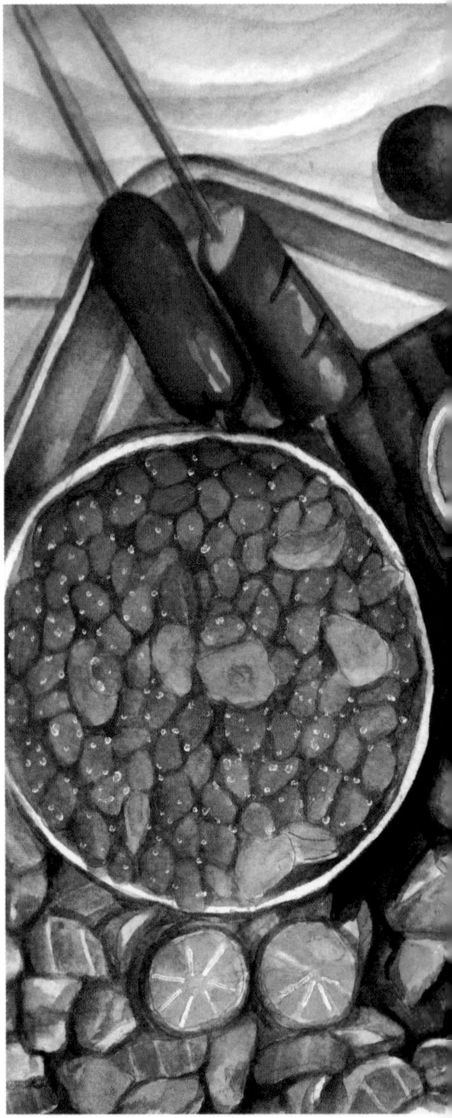

Dílis at Adóbong Manî

/Dí·lis/ & /A·dó·bong Ma·nî/

Dílis is an anchovy about the length of a matchstick. As *pulútan*, it is dried and salted then coated in chili-laced sugar and fried. Its perfect partner is *manî* (peanut) made into an *adóbo*. It is seasoned with vinegar, lots of salt, a good measure of black pepper, and chili, whether *síling labúyo*, *pasíti*, or *habà*.

Sísig

/Sí·sig/

Fatty pork ear, cheek, tail, and a full head of skin are boiled till soft, then grilled until crisp. Originally a dish for pregnant women nearing delivery, *sísig* is the drinker's darling, perked up by onion, chili, and *kalamansí*. When served on a sizzling platter, *sísig* may have a raw egg on top meant for mixing in.

Salpikáw

/Sal·pi·káw/

Garlic is the dominant flavor in this dish of soft, beef tenderloin tips. Soy sauce is the commonly used salter, and mushrooms are sometimes added. *Salpikáw* is a *pulútan* that can be considered high-end. It may not be available at beach and roadside bars or if it is, less expensive cuts of beef will be used.

Tókwa't Báboy

/Tók·wa't Bá·boy/

Bite-sized cubes of *tókwa* (firm soybean curd) and *báboy* (pork) make *tókwa't báboy* (literally firm soybean curd and pork). Fatty parts of the pig such as *máskará* (literally "mask," but meaning head skin) and belly are essential for *pulútan*. Other ingredients of the dish are tomato, onion, garlic, black pepper, chili, ginger, vinegar, sugar, and soy sauce.

Nógada de Págì

/Nó·ga·da de Pá·gi/

Popular in the San Roque district of Cavite is a dish of *pági* (young honeycomb stingray) cooked with beer, miso, *quesillo* (carabao milk cheese), salted duck egg, and *wansúy* (native coriander). Supposedly, it got its name from the way the cheese and the miso mix into sauce, resembling walnut cream. *Nógada* is Spanish for walnut tree.

Crispy Crablets

In the Philippines, crabs half the length of a thumb are turned into deep-fried, crunchy chow that should be dipped in vinegar made piquant with raw white and red onion, chili and raw ginger. The Lilliputian crablets are best enjoyed straight from the cooking pan. But remember, they are a seasonal find.

Pang-Pistá

/Pang-Pis·tá/

Festival Food

Holidays and holy days give Filipinos their calendar of fiestas by which to sustain a collective, multi-cultural memory and identity. Overdoing the eating and the drinking conscientiously is one way to guarantee that a fiesta is no ordinary day. Families aim to serve only the best local delicacies around. There are master cooks and even caterers specializing in special fiesta needs. Predominantly, a form of legacy cooking, fiesta meals are also when new favorite foods and homemade specialties appear at table. Meat dishes, colored rice, and sweets that require tedious preparation characterize festival fare. Today, however, one can have fiesta foods every day because restaurants offer them.

Pagána Mëranaw

/Pa·gá·na Më·ra·naw/

The Mëranaw are an ethnolinguistic group who peopled Mindanao. They converted to Islam before Europeans brought Christianity to the Philippines. A *pagána* with its splendid gold-colored theme is their meal during celebrations. Food is served to guests on a stack of *tábak* (footed brass tray), each covered with a colorful *ampás* cloth. Sweets like small *brówa* (cakes), durian-filled *dódol* (sweets), and threadlike *tiyátug* (wafers), *paborót* (ground sticky rice), and *tamokónsi* (soft dough pretzel) fill saucers on the bottom tier. The middle *tábak* has *koníng* (turmeric rice) decorated with hard-boiled eggs. On the top tier are plates of chicken, carabao or beef, and bowls of soup flavored with curries and *palápa* (spice mixtures).

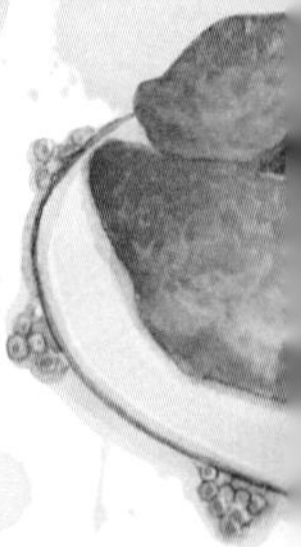

Pabo

Tábak

Dód

Tiyátug

Koníng

Tamokonsi

Yu
Siopac
Vegetables

Peking Duck

Tíkoy

Chinese Lunar New Year

Tsinóy is the affectionate term created for Filipinos (*Pinóys* in street jargon) who keep their Chinese (*Tsíno*) ancestry alive. They serve *yu* (a fish complete with head and tail), at the start of the new lunar year because the word sounds like a term for richness and surplus. Duck, usually roasted, symbolizes fidelity. Shrimp stands for happiness. Noodles bring long life and should never be cut while eating them. Vegetables cleanse the body. Everyone eats sweet, sticky *tíkoy* (rice cake) to keep the Kitchen God's mouth shut and unable to reveal a family's bad behavior during the past year. *Tíkoy* comes in uniquely *Tsinóy* flavors, such as *pandán* (fragrant screwpine) and *úbe* (purple yam).

Noodles

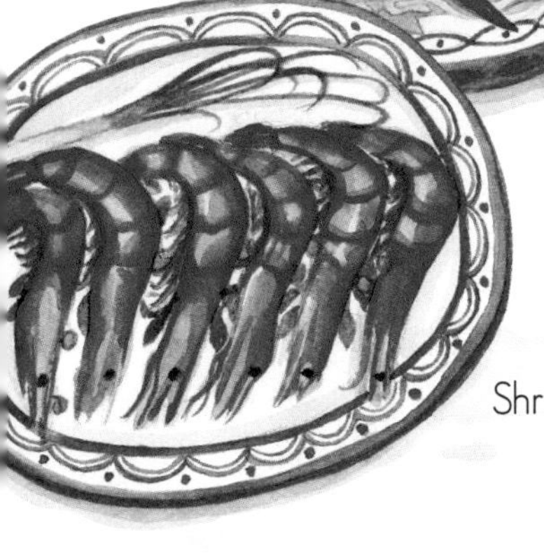

Shrimp

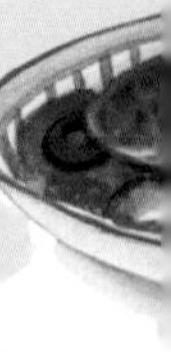

Pistá ng Báyan

/Pis·tá ng Bá·yan/
Town Festival

Morcón

Pistá ng báyan commonly refers to a town's celebration recollecting a Roman Catholic saint after whom the parish is named, or a Biblical event shared by all Catholics such as Christmas and Easter. A *lechón* (spit-roasted whole pig), large enough to feed clan and guests, stars on the menu. Golden *arróz a la valenciánia* and *brínghe* (similar to paella), *léngua* (ox tongue) stewed with Spanish sausage and banana, *morcón* (beef roulade) filled with ground pork and Edam cheese, *pastél de pólyo* (chicken pie) with *dáyap* (native lime) and soy sauce, as well as fancy sweets like egg-rich *yéma* (a native dessert made of egg yolk and condensed milk coated with sugar or hardened caramelized sugar) or *tocíno del cielo* (rich custared made with egg yolk, butter and sugar) or rice-based *sapín-sapín* or *palitáw* share top billing.

Tocíno del cielo

Yéma

Lechón

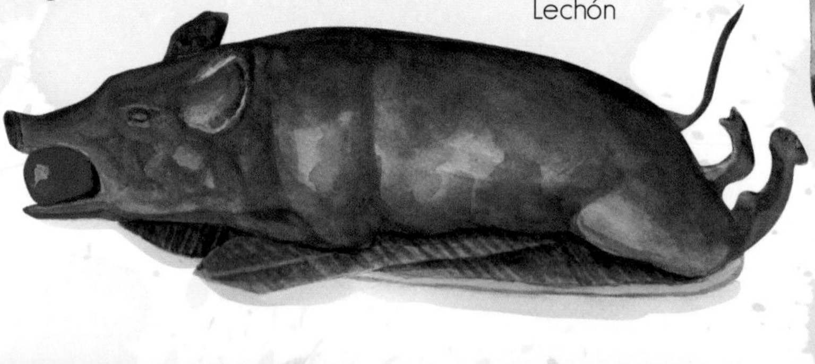

Pastél de pólyo
Léngua
Arróz a la valenciánia
Sapín-sapín

Inúmin

/I·nú·min/

Drinks

Keeping hydrated is vital in a hot, humid, tropical climate like that of the Philippines. Coconut water, quaffed straight out of a nut, is nature's health drink to supplement fresh water. The age-old rule, "Fresh is fantastic" holds true when enjoying fruit juices and shakes. Chilled was the pre-ice-cold custom; cooling drinks in a stream creates a lasting memory when in a Philippine waterscape. Beverages include local palm and rice wines, as well as internationally awarded, locally distilled rums, coconut vodkas, beers, and fruit liqueurs. Cacao was introduced from Mexico when it was a Spanish colony. Coffee came too, becoming a Philippine export.

10 PHP
ELON
10 PHP
BUKO
CE
UBE MACAPUNO
BUKO PA
MANGO JUICE
COFFEE JELLY
HALO - HALO

Búko Juice

/Bú·ko Jus/

A must-have is water straight from *búko*, a young coconut with delectably tender flesh. It is naturally sweet and refreshing even when not chilled. Ripe and unripe mango, *melón* (cantaloupe), *guyabáno* (soursop), and *dúhat* (Java Plum) are among many fruits made into juices and shakes. "Fresh" is a remarkable revelation, so characteristic of the best Philippine foods and beverages.

Sagó't Guláman

/Sa·gó't Gu·lá·man/

Guláman, also known as *ágar-ágar*, is gelatin made from seaweed and does not need refrigeration to solidify. Cut into small cubes, it is served with pea-size *sagó* (tapioca) in water flavored by aromatic *pandán* (fragrant screwpine) and raw sugar syrup. It may be chilled or iced. Adding coconut milk increases its yumminess.

Tsokoláte at Kapé

/Tso·ko·lá·te/ & /Ka·pé/

Tsokoláte (chocolate) is made the antique way: using hand-ground roasted cacao beans that are sweetened and served so thick a biscuit can stand in it. Water or carabao milk are used to thin it. Davao-grown cacao beans have been winning international awards. Philippine *kapé* (coffee) includes lauded varieties of *barákο* and Arabica; costly Civet Coffee is also produced.

Halò-Halò

/Ha·lò-Ha·lò/ or /Ha·lú-Ha·lò/

Halò-Halò is the most colorful and, perhaps, the happiest drink. *Halo* means "to mix" and *halò-halò* implies "very mixed." Banana, *káong* (palm seeds), coconut rashers, chickpea, bean, and flan sweetened in syrup, *guláman*, and *halayáng úbe* (purple yam jam) are piled on shaved or crushed ice. Evaporated milk completes the toppings. A scoop of ice-cream crowns *Halò-halò Éspesyál*.

BASI

Básì, Lambanóg, Tubâ, at Tápuy

/Bá·si, /Lam·ba·nóg/, /Tu·bâ/, & /Tá·puy/

Native liquors are part of the local party scene. Beware! They are potent. *Básì* is made from sugarcane, *lambanóg* and *tubâ* from coconut, *tápuy* from rice. They are taken straight, on the rocks, or mixed into tropical cocktails. Family recipes strengthen alcoholic potency by curing prunes and raisins in bottles of liquor buried underground for use at special events.

Sa Panaderyá

/Pa·na·der·yá/

Bakery Finds

Philippine breads, biscuits, cakes, crackers, cookies, muffins, and pies are made mostly of wheat flour, but also of arrowroot, potato, and rice flours. In addition to factory brands, neighborhood bakeries and specialty shops provide favorites and new varieties too many of them to keep track of. Spanish settlers introduced the beehive oven and the roasting of flat breads over an open fire. Chinese immigrants brought the knowledge of how to make breads by steaming. While some breads are intentionally soft, there also are crisp, dense, double-baked breads called *biskótso* (biscócho) that are the delicious off-spring of hard-as-rock sea biscuit carried as sustenance on galleons.

Pacéncia

/Pa·cén·cia/ or /Pa·sén·si·ya/

Paciencia, meaning "patience", is a meringue-like biscuit, round, and dainty as a button. Egg whites and sugar are its main ingredients. One wonders if the product is named after a quality needed by every baker who had to hand whisk the whites till they stood at attention. One *pacéncia*, even a handful, is never enough to satisfy a craving for them.

Hojáldres

/Ho·jál·dres/

Hojáldres are sugar-sprinkled biscuits made of puff pastry, quite like sweet, crisp *palmiers*. They are perfect with a cup of coffee, provided they do not shatter in your fingers first as they are fragile. A sturdier version of the cookie is the *ótap* of Cebu. Philippines *hojáldres* was made with *sébo* (pork fat) when there was no imported butter.

Úbe bread

Úbe Cake

/Ú·be Kéyk/

Úbe (purple yam) colors cakes that tower primly or roll around creamy filling. It is one of many soft-eating cakes such as *tórtang Cebu*, *taisán* (*taysán*), and *mamón*. Cakes for birthdays and weddings can be quite an experience, unbelievably ornate and meticulously hand decorated. *Úbe*, a popular flavoring, appears in pancake, breads, Chinese tea-cakes, and rice cakes alike.

Búko Pie

/Bú·ko Páy/

It is a lidded pie with a filling of tender ribbons of *búko* (young coconut). In Los Baños, a town south of Metro Manila known for hot springs, many bakeries claim to be the pie's inventor. The pie is also made in Bacolod and other areas where coconut is grown. It is outstanding when served a la mode.

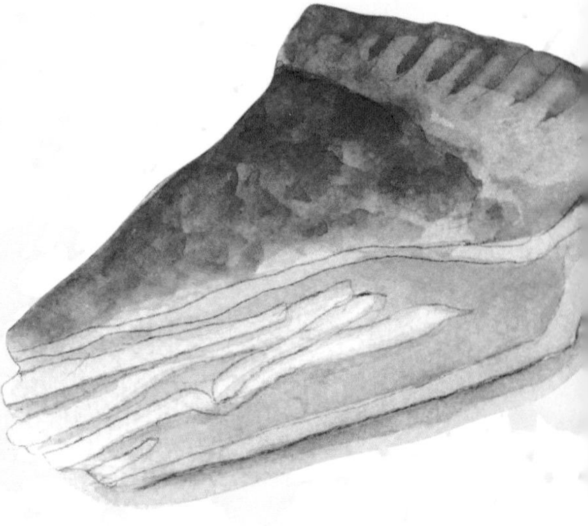

Rosquíllos

/Ros·kíl·yos/

Rosquíllo means "ringlet" in Spanish, which describes the appearance of these crisp treats. The yellow-colored biscuit is made with shortening, flour, sugar, baking powder and eggs. Margarita "Titay" T. Frasco invented a *rosquíllo* in 1907 in Liloan, Cebu and the recipe is still kept secret by her family. Recipes of 1919 add anise, sesame seeds, and a white icing.

Gallétas

/Gal·yé·tas/

Gallétas are thin, sand-toned discs of pastry, sometimes with a fluted edge. They are neutral on the palate, not at all sugary, and so are especially good with a mug of sweetened coffee or tea. They typify a wide range of traditional *biskwít* (biscuit or cracker) that include *gallétas de huévos* (eggs) and *de patátas* (potatoes, although not an ingredient).

Tórta

/Tór·ta/

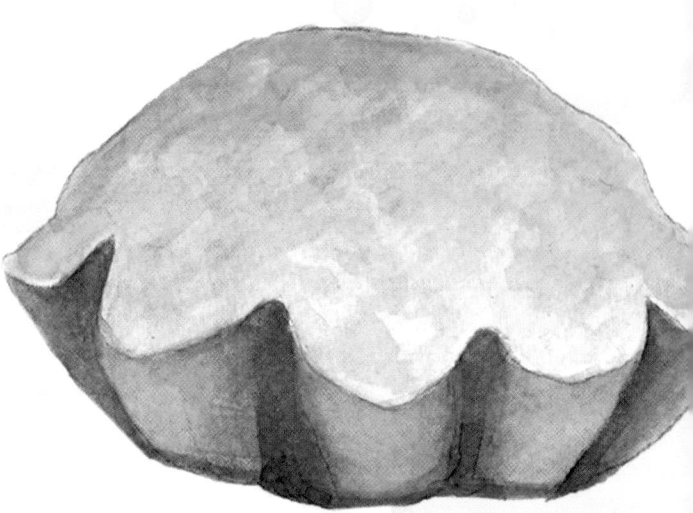

Tórta is a small cake made in the Visayas. In Cebu, it has a texture somewhere in between a brioche and a butter cake. Its batter is leavened with *tubâ* or coconut wine, enriched with egg yolks, and made with pork lard. Argao, Carcar, Cebu City, and Liloan flavor *tórta* with fragrant aniseed. Although available daily, it is a fiesta celebrity.

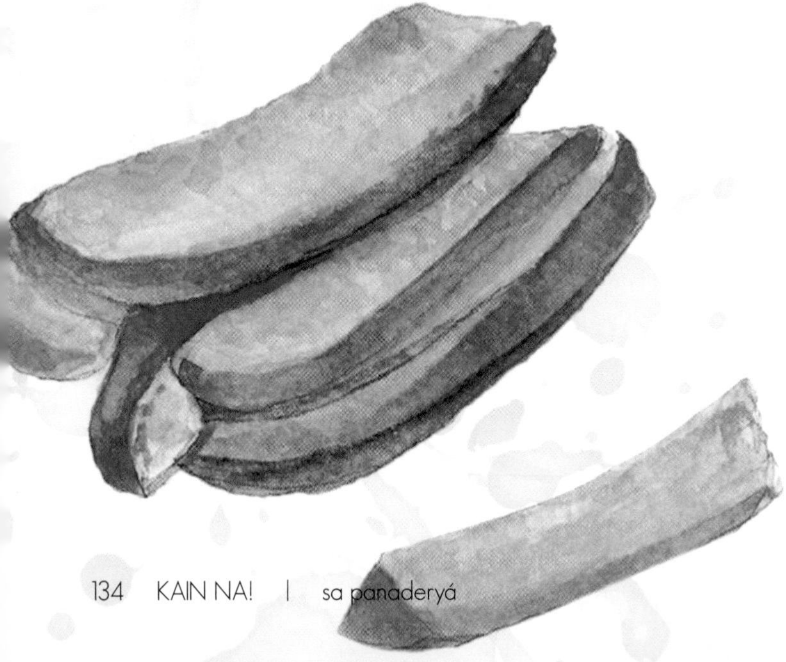

Biscócho

/Bis·kót·so/

Biscócho is twice-baked bread. At its best, *biscócho* leaves no crumbs with every bite because it is finely textured, densely packed leaving no air space, and baked till dry. It is a sweetish, textural complement to accompany a soup, a moist noodle stir-fry, or a cup of chocolate. *Biscócho de cáña* resembles a *cáña* (bamboo cane) sliced lengthwise and naturally curved.

Uraró

/U·ra·ró/

Uraro means "arrowroot", whose flour is the chief ingredient for these airy, tender, melt-in-the-mouth biscuits. They are shaped using molds of different designs, such as small stars, ridged discs, or flowers. They may be wrapped in squares of thin paper known as *papél de Hapón* or gingerly, neatly, packed into plastic jars.

Kalíhim

/Ka·lí·him/

Known by its sweet, red, custard filling, *kalíhim* (secretary) is also called "lipstick bread" and, with a touch of black humor, *pán de régla* (bread of menstruation). Perhaps it is called *kalíhim* that also means "secret," because it holds a bakery trade's confidence: it is the result of recycling. The custard is made with crushed leftover bread.

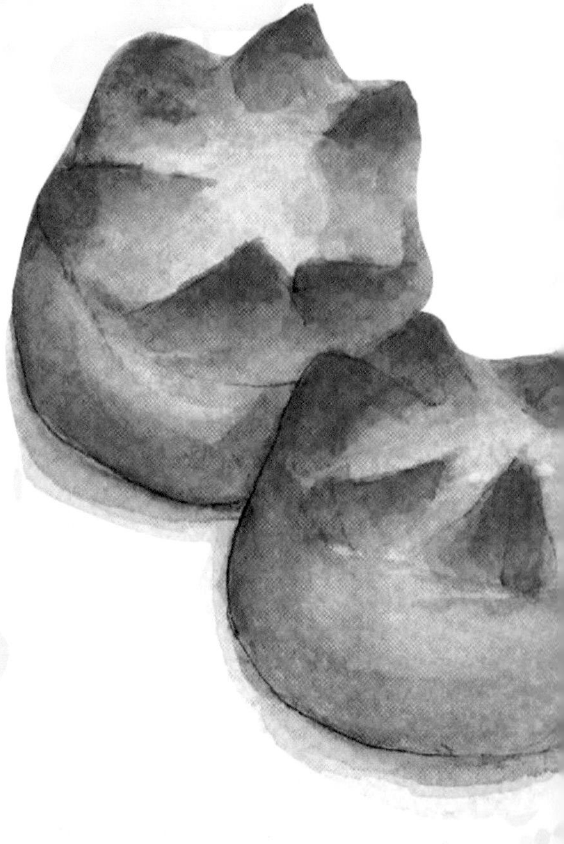

Putók

/Pu·tók/

Pán de sál (bread of salt) is the beloved Filipino daily bread, a cultural culinary icon. Often it has a crack on one side, giving it a second name, *pán de putók* (bread of a burst or an explosion). *Pán de sál* was first used locally as a measure of solid, not granulated, salt. The bun was simply called *pán*, then.

Spánish Bread

/Spánish Bread/

Spanish Bread has no Spanish name in the Philippines, only an English one. Could that hint at the bread roll's relative newness? Whatever its origin, Spanish Bread is popular and varied around the islands. The most common filling is a moist spread of margarine, sugar, powdered milk, and breadcrumbs. It can be topped with margarine that makes it glow golden.

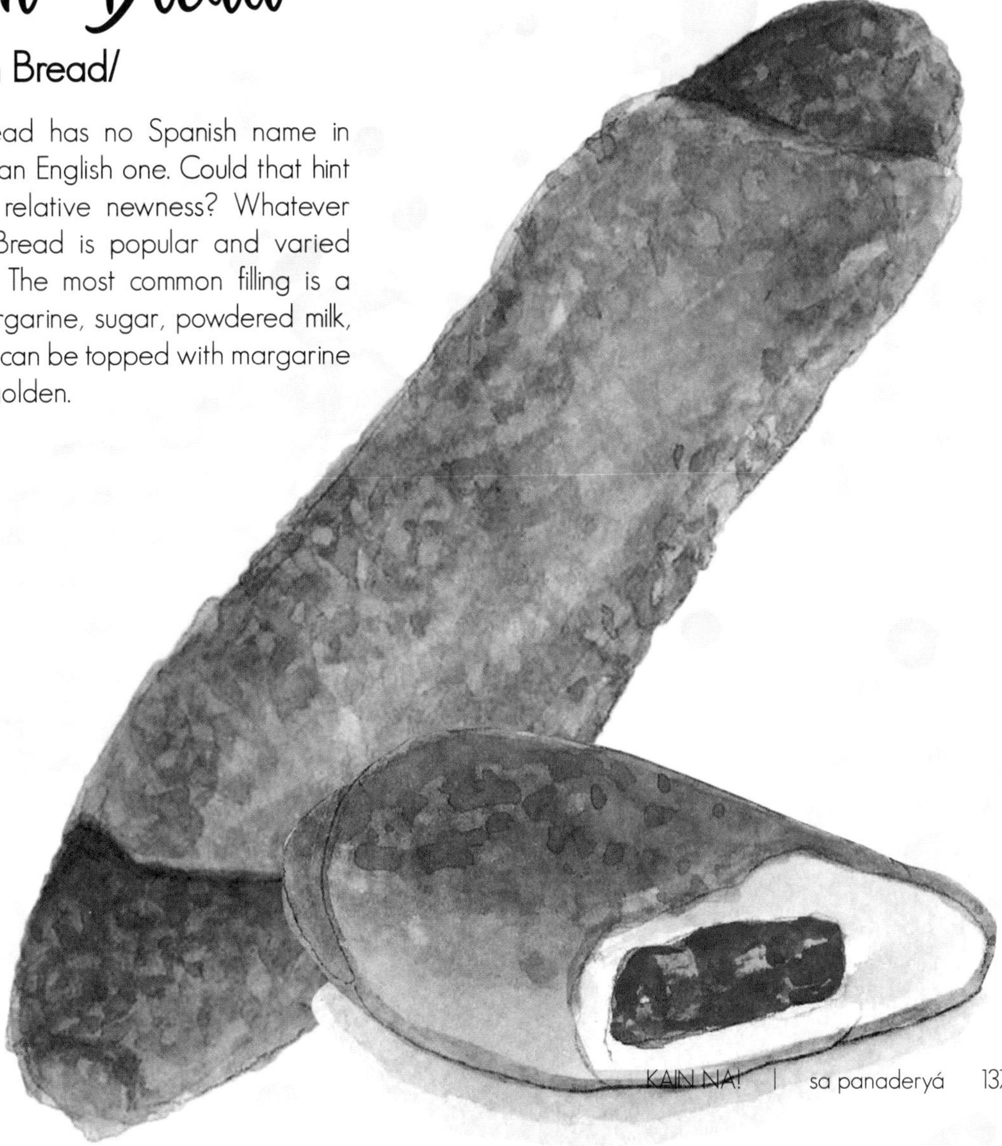

Pán de Cóco

/Pán de Có·co/

Pán de Cóco (bread of coconut) lives up to its name by having a filling of desiccated coconut mixed with *kalamansí* (native lemon) rind, brown sugar, and margarine. The same dough is used for breads with other sweet stuffing such as *makapunò* (coconut sport), red mongo bean, pounded boiled peanut, *úbe* jam, or glazed fruits.

Mónay

/Mó·nay/

Mónay means both a kind of bread and the similarly shaped bun women make of their hair. Every dense loaf, whether fist-small or as large as a dinner plate, is divided by a slash into two sections. Folk joke that *mónay* resembles a woman's plump bottom and its original name may have been *pán de mónja* (nun's bread).

Pinóy Tasty

/Pi·nóy Téys·ti/

Tasty is machine-sliced sandwich loaf that likely is the soft, native interpretation of Tastee, a brand famous in the United States during the early 1900s. The bread has Tastee's innovative flattened top that was practical for loading in the large volumes needed to serve train passengers on Pullman cars that the loaf's shape coincidentally resembles.

Kababáyan

/Ka·ba·bá·yan/

The small, sweet, moist, dense, and golden-brown cupcake known as *kababáyan* has a characteristic center dome or hump. Somewhat sticky when bit, it is made with evaporated milk and margarine. *Kababáyan* means compatriot, those sharing the same bayan (country or community). It is also called *kabáyan* (short for *kababáyan*) and *kaláhi* (those of the same race).

Kakanín

/Ka·ka·nín/

Rice Cakes

Rice is central to Philippine cuisine and culture. There are thousands of rice varieties that come in different colors, shapes, and even fragrances. Ancestors believed each grain had a soul commanding respect and careful handling. Sticky rice varieties were preferred as pagan offerings. They continue as special occasion cakes and puddings as well as daily comfort foods. When eaten wisely, rice is a healthy source of lasting energy. While *kakanín* takes its name from *kánin* (cooked rice), it can be made from root crops like cassava and sweet potato. Wheat flour finds its way into many of them now bringing down the price and ease of making *kakanín*.

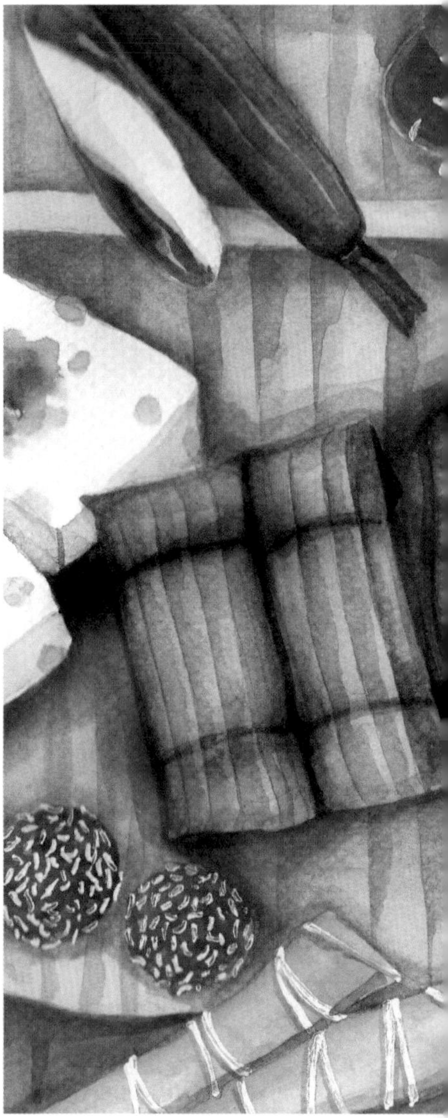

Súman

/Sú·man/

Súman is a class of *kakanín* with many variations. Finger-long *súman sa íbus* is wrapped like a mummy in buri palm leaves (*íbus*). *Súman* in Ilokos, called *súman inángit*, is swaddled in banana leaf; in Baler, in coconut leaf; in Leyte and Samar where it is pyramidal, in *hagíkhik* leaf. *Súman sa lihíya* is made with *lihíya* (lye).

Súman Morón

/Sú·man Mo·rón/

In Leyte and Samar, this *súman* is made with ground rice instead of whole glutinous grain. The rice flour is cooked into a paste with sugar and coconut milk. Small cakes of ground, roasted chocolate for cooking into beverage are crushed and used as the core of an elongated *súman* made with the flour or mixed in for a marbled effect.

Púto

/Pú·to/

The varieties of *púto*, steamed rice cake, escape counting. They are airy, sticky, or gelatinous. Some are over a foot wide or bite-size, like *Pútong polo* from Bulacan. *Púto manapla*, named after its Negros Occidental hometown, is flavored by *sabá* banana leaf. Steamed in bamboo tubes is *púto bumbóng* of purplish *pirurútong* rice and once sold only around Christmas.

Palitáw

/Pa·li·táw/

Finest rice flour and water are made into small flat cakes, then submerged in boiling water. When cooked they float, thus their name from *litáw* (to appear). *Palitáw* is eaten with grated fresh coconut meat, raw or white sugar and sesame seeds. The beverage to pair with it is *salabát*, a tisane of fresh ginger root.

Tibòk-Tibòk

/Ti·bòk-Ti·bòk/

An exquisite, firm, sweet pudding that combines luxuriant carabao milk and scrumptious coconut cream, *tibòk-tibòk* quivers like a heartbeat, thus its name. A hint of *dáyap* (native lime) zest keeps the richness in check. Rice flour thickens this jewel of a *kakanín* from Pampanga that is essential for the fiesta menu.

Sapin-Sapin

/Sa·pín-Sa·pín/

One *sapín* (pad) after another of coconut cream, rice flour, and sugar is steamed and stacked to make colorful *sapín-sapín*. Traditionally the base is white, the middle golden from annatto, and the top purple *halayáng úbe* (purple yam jam). Malabon in Metro Manila adds corn to one pad. A topping of *latík* (coconut curd) adds textural counterpoint.

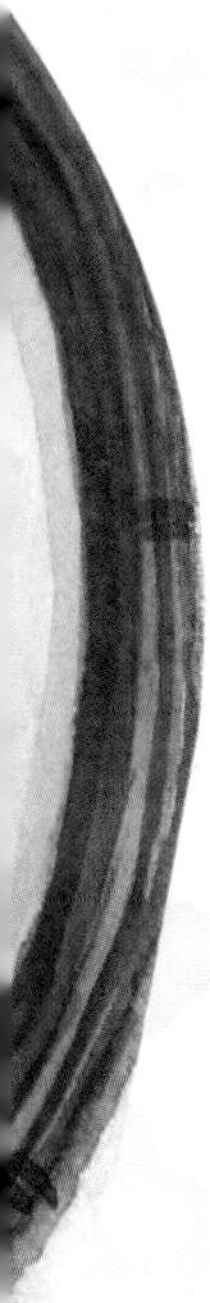

Bíko

/Bí·ko/

Bíko is made by cooking steamed glutinous rice with sugar and coconut cream to produce a thick, swollen mass. It is taken as is or topped with reduced coconut cream called *latík*. In Laguna, a southern Luzon province, *bíko* is called *sinúkmánì*.

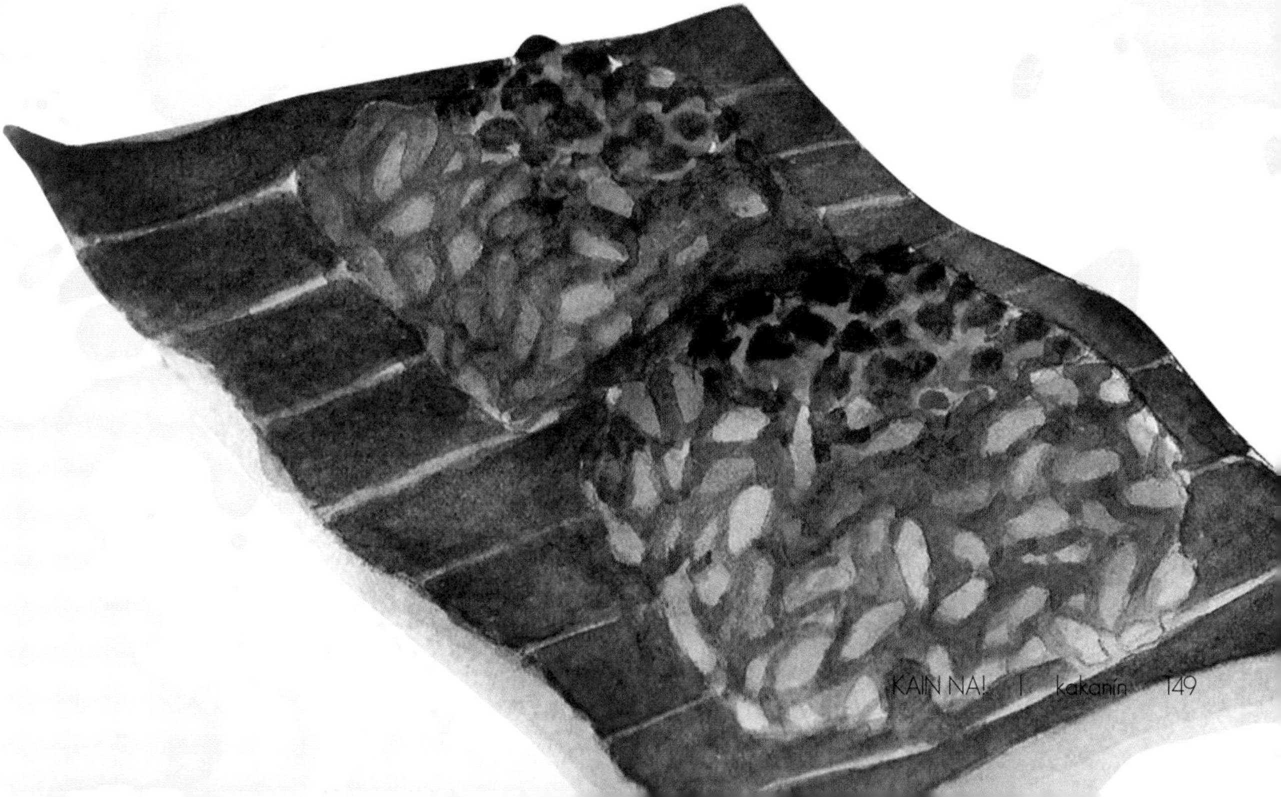

Patúpat

/Pa·tú·pat/

Patúpat comes from the Ilokos. Soaked and drained glutinous rice is packed into woven basket-like parcels of coconut blade. Clusters of them are immersed into woks of boiling sugar cane molasses and coconut cream until the grains within are soft, dark amber, and sweet.

Túpig

/Tú·pig/

A specialty from Ilokos is *túpig*, a *kakanín* commonly grilled or baked in embers. The favorite *kakanín* is an elongated banana leaf parcel filled with a gloopy batter of ground glutinous rice, coconut milk, sugar, and shredded, tender *búko* (young coconut).

Píchi-Píchi

/Pí·chi-Pí·chi/

Píchi-píchi are steamed, quivering, translucent cakes of grated cassava and sugar. *Lihíya* (lye) is sometimes added for a bit of crunch. They are often rolled in grated coconut and grated cheese. Quezon Province claims the *píchi-píchi* was invented there.

Kutsintâ

/Kut·sin·tâ/

Kutsintâ is made with a very liquid batter of annatto water, brown sugar, rice flour and *lihíya* (lye). This batter is divided among little cups or poured into a mould and then steamed until they are translucent and a dark, reddish brown. Sometimes spelled as *cuchintâ*, the wobbly little cakes are eaten with grated coconut.

Binállay at Moriécos

/Bi·nál·lay/ & /Mor·yé·cos/

Both *kakanín* are found in Luzon's provinces of Aurora and Isabela. *Binállay* are oblong banana leaf parcels of coconut milk, sugar, and glutinous rice flour. These steamed dumplings are enjoyed with rivers of red *latík* (coconut caramel sauce) and were traditional only during Holy Week. *Moriécos* is similar but contains grated coconut cooked with *panocha* (*panutsá*) (unrefined cane or coconut sugar).

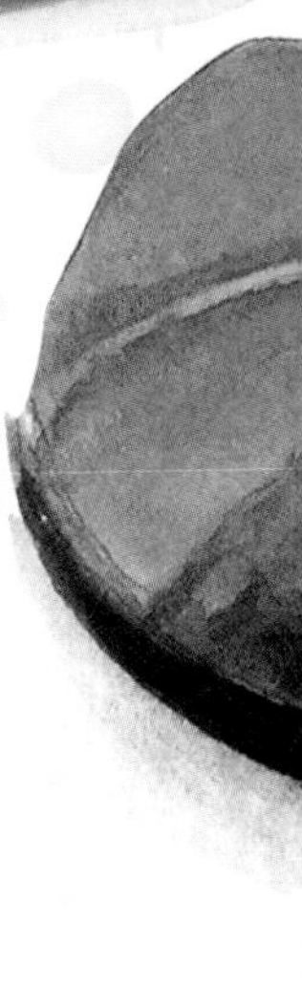

Binagól

/Bi·na·gól/

Binagól is a specialty of Dagami, Leyte. It is made with grated *talyán*, a kind of taro root that is cooked with sugar, coconut cream, egg yolk, condensed milk, and peanut before being stuffed into coconut shells covered with banana leaf for boiling in water. The word *binagól* comes from *bagól*, meaning "coconut shell" in Waray, the language of Leyte.

Dúman

/Dú·man/

Dúman is unripe glutinous rice of a certain variety, hand beaten to remove husks from grains that are then toasted. Grown solely in Pampanga's Sta. Rita town, the little amount harvested is only available in November. The labor-intensive processing makes it expensive. *Dúman* is stirred into mugs of chocolate or cooked with coconut cream for a kind of *bíko* or *súman*.

Puttì Mandì

/Put·lì Man·dì/

A Tausug delicacy from the ethnic group of the Sulu archipelago, *putlì mandì* is a little orb stuffed with *hínti* (grated coconut cooked with sugar). Its skin is made with either ground purple glutinous rice or ordinary ground rice tinted with purple food dye. A batch of the cooked, boiled dumpling is then rolled in fresh or toasted grated coconut.

Bícho-Bícho

/Bí·cho-Bí·cho/ /Bít·so-Bít·so/

They are fritters made with a dough of ground glutinous rice, wheat flour, *búko* (young coconut), and coconut cream. After being shaped to the cook's preference, a *bícho-bícho* is boiled and deep-fried until golden. The cooked fritters are usually tossed in bubbling *latík*, (coconut caramel sauce) that makes them doubly scrumptious. They are best consumed immediately while hot, but not piping.

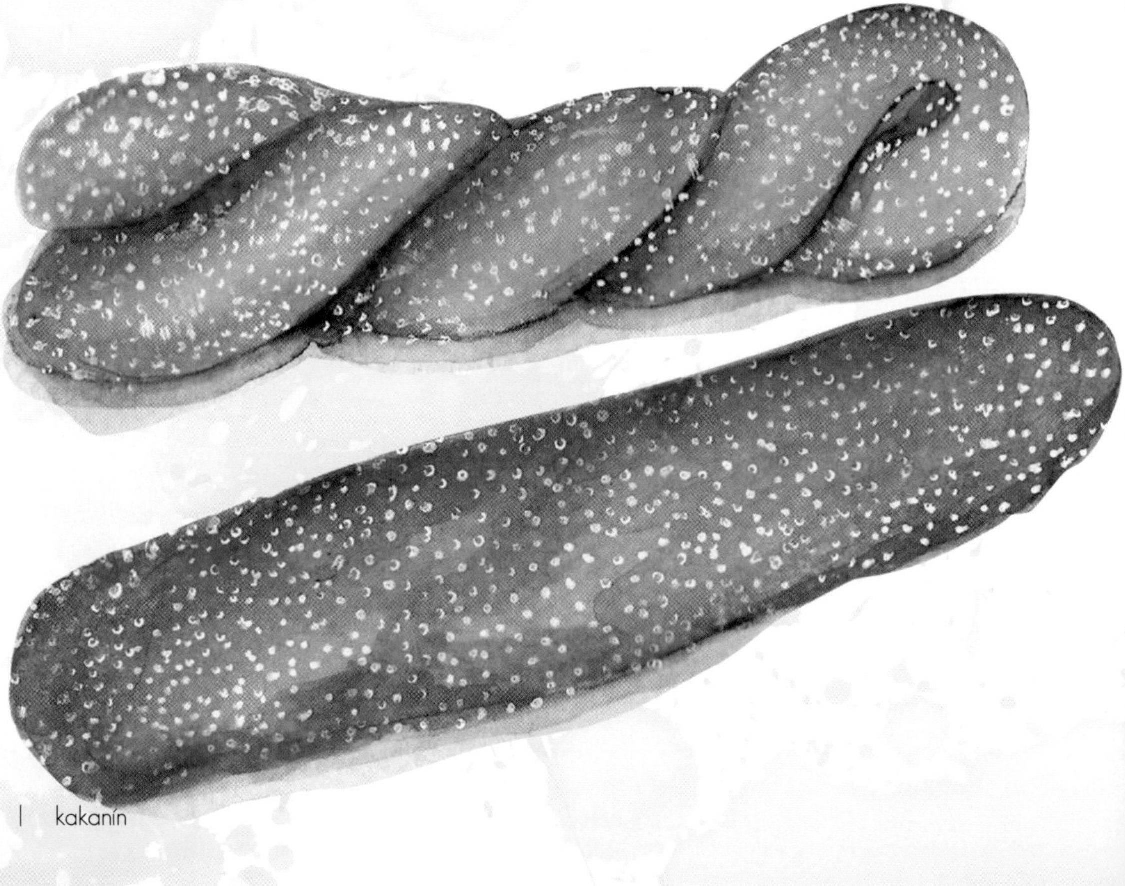

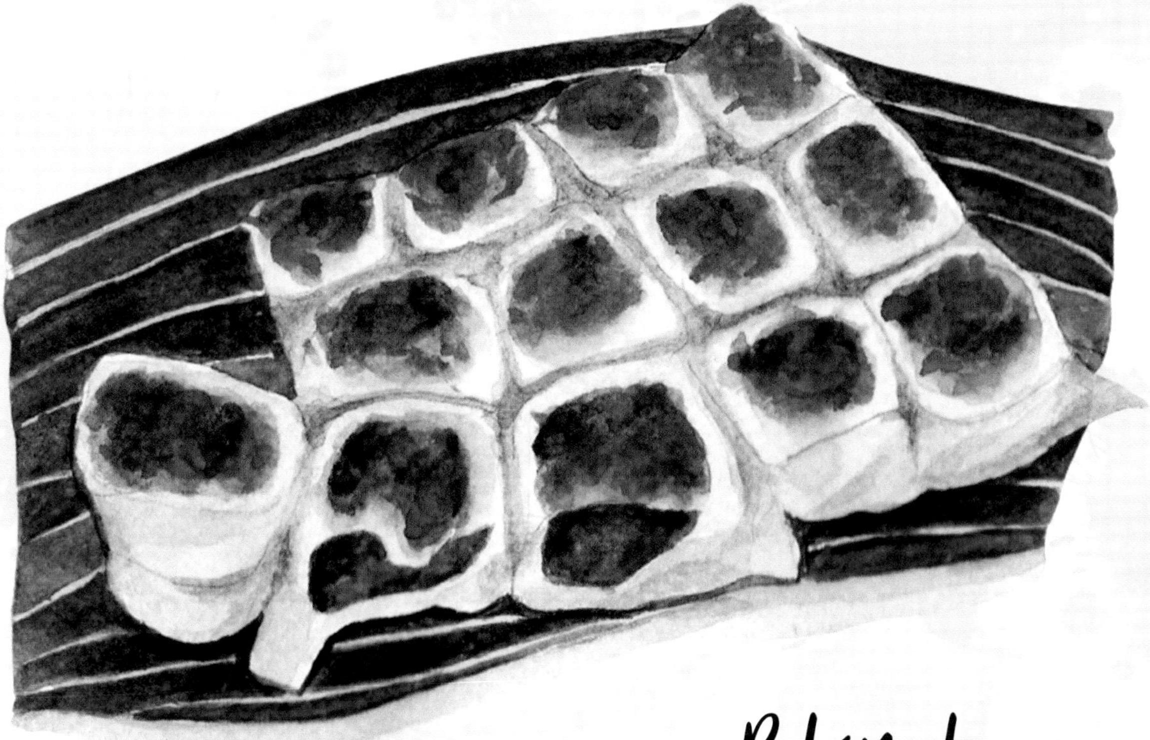

Bibíngkoy

/Bi·bíng·koy/

Bibíngkoy is a Caviteño delicacy involving buns made from glutinous rice flour. They are stuffed with crushed, lightly sweetened red bean. The cakes are crammed onto a vast tray and grilled. Snipped-out servings are draped with a thick coconut sauce sometimes flavored by jackfruit and studded with *sagó* pearls. The delight is named after *bibíngka,* an oven-baked rice cake.

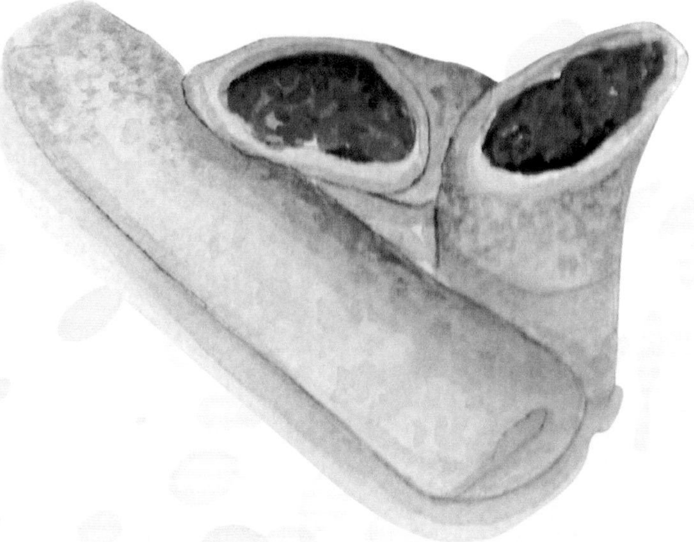

Darál

/Da·rál/

Darál is a fine crepe made with rice flour, coconut cream, and egg by ethnic groups of Mindanao that include Tausug, Joloan, and Subanon. Before rolling up, a thin, cooked crepe is filled with sticky *hínti* (grated coconut cooked with sugar). Some contemporary interpretations are made with wheat flour thickening the crepe and bestowing it a pancake-like texture.

Aripahól

/A·ri·pa·hól/

Aripahól is made with grated cassava mixed with sugar packed into coconut husks lined with brown sugar, and then steamed. It is crucial that the grated cassava is thoroughly dried, preferably under the sun, as excess moisture will produce a dense and heavy cake. It is a Western Visayas specialty, where it is also known as *púto lansón*.

Salukarâ

/Sa·lu·ka·râ/

This simple, tender little crepe hails from Eastern Samar and Leyte. It is made with ground rice, sugar, coconut milk, and *tubâ* (coconut wine) that serves as a leavening agent. It is usually served folded to resemble a triangle and is enjoyed eaten with *latík* (coconut caramel syrup). Quite enjoyable, one *salukarâ* is never enough.

Bayé- Bayé

/Ba·yé-Ba·yé/

It is made by pounding young rice with almost-mature coconut and sugar, and then shaping the resulting dough into rolls. It is a product of Pavia town in Iloilo. Another version is shaped into small balls made with white, glutinous corn, shredded coconut, and brown sugar; it can be eaten with *lupák* (a sweet paste of banana and coconut).

Dinumúgan

/Di·nu·mú·gan/

It is a type of *súman* from Bohol made of crushed *sabá* (cooking banana), grated *lukarón* (teenage coconut), ground rice, and sugar. The *sabá* has to be almost overripe for the *kakanín*'s unique flavor to shine through. Philippine preparations have a range of natural sweetness depending on when ingredients are harvested and may not need the additional sprinkling of granulated sugar.

Búdbud Kabòg

/Búd·bud Ka·bòg/

Búdbud is the Cebuano word for *súman. Kabòg* is millet, a cereal grown in Cebu before the Spanish arrived in the 16th century. To make into *búdbud*, millet is cooked with sugar and coconut milk into a gruel that is then rolled up in banana leaves and boiled. *Bíngka dáwa* has a fine texture because it uses *kabòg* ground into flour.

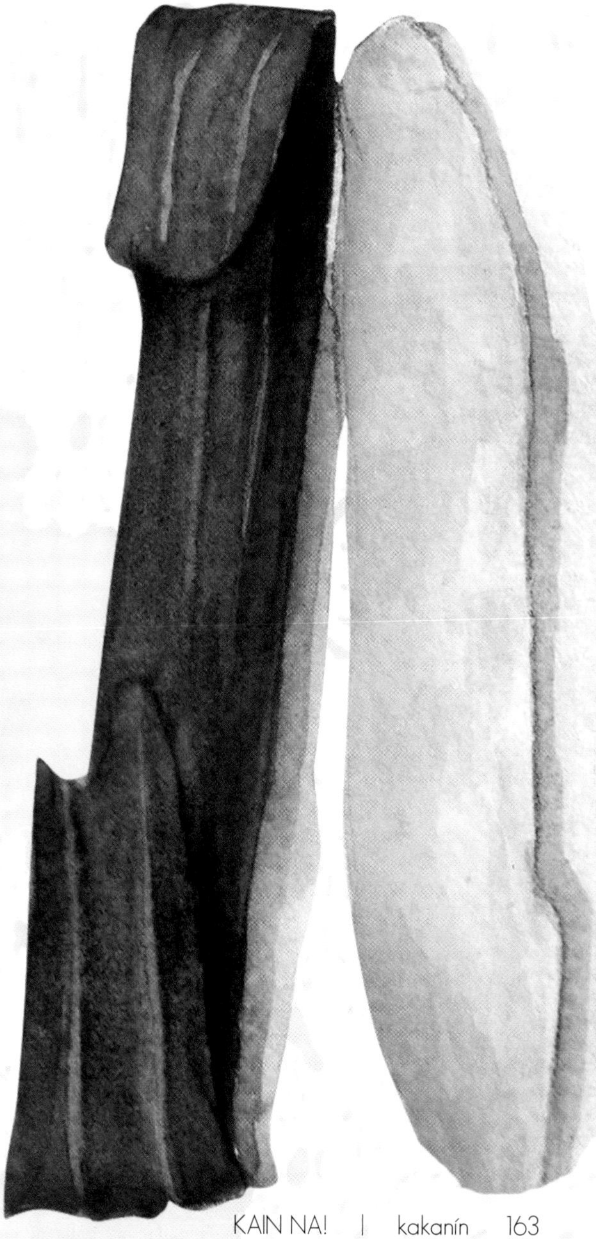

Mga Sawsáwan

/Saw·sá·wan/

Dips & Sauces

Master cooks are lauded for their signature savors throughout the archipelago. But the local culture encourages each one at the table to adjust even the best dish to suit the changing, even fickle moods of taste buds. The goal is *malinamnám* (deliciousness), by balancing flavors as one sees fit. Mix and match tastes and textures of sauces, relishes, and mashes with one's menu. Pineapple is eaten with salt. Smoked, salted beef may need a sweet mango on the side. Perk up a meal's mood mid-way with a chili-punctuated soy sauce or artisanal vinegar dip. The everyday Philippine meal is participative, interactive, and meant to be personalized as one desires.

Pampaálat

/Pam·pa·á·lat/

Alat means salty. *Bagoóng*, a naturally fermented seafood paste, has a liquid by-product called *patís*. *Bagoóng alamáng* is made with tiniest shrimp; *Batangueño bagoóng baláyan*, fish; Ilocano *monamon*, anchovy. *Patís* can be thick, dark, and earthy, or amber, light, and silky on the tongue. *Tóyo* is fermented soya bean sauce. They are all *pampaálat* (salters for cooking), and table use.

PATIS
TOYO

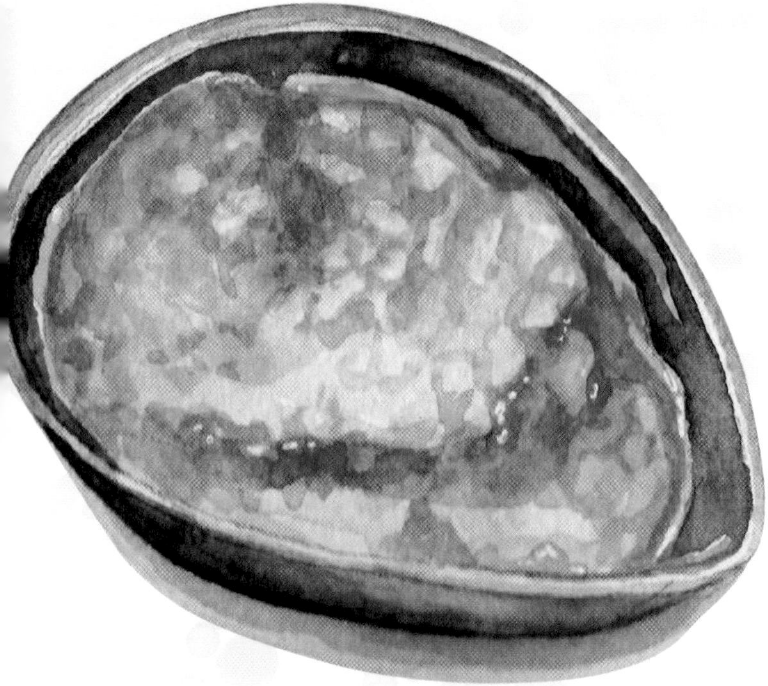

Búro

/Bú·ro/

Búro means brined. One variety is an annatto-colored mix of fermented fish, shrimp, or pork with salt and rice. It is sautéed with garlic and eaten as part of a main meal. *Búrong manggá* (brined unripe mango, especially the thumb-size paho variety) and *búrong labanós* (brined radish) are made into mashes. *Maálat na itlóg* (salted duck egg) is minced with fresh tomato for textural staccato.

Pampaásim

/Pam·pa·á·sim/

The juices of *dáyap* (native lime) and *kalamansí* (native lemon), *kamyás* (bilimbi) slices, and *súka* (vinegar) add *ásim* (sourness) to dishes at the table. Towns are proud of their small-batch vinegars. They are made from *nípa* in Paombong; *lubí* (coconut) or *bulí* (raffia) in Bohol and Cebu; pineapple in Tagaytay. Iloilo's *sinamák* and Misamis Occidental's *pinakurát* are vinegars with chili that can strike like lightning.

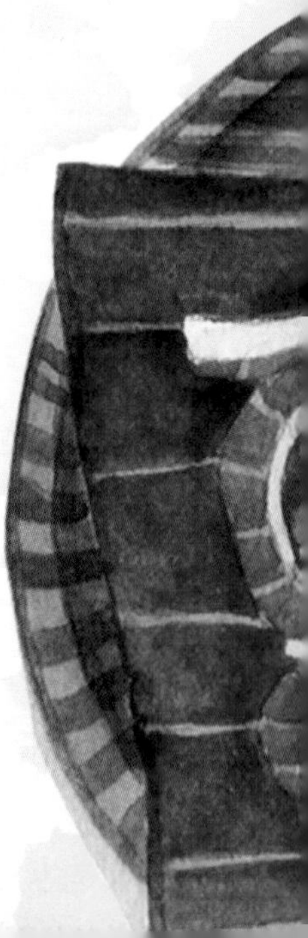

Asín

/A·sín/

Asín (salt) is harvested as rough grains from the sea using natural evaporation in the sun. Salt flakes in Pangasinan are from salt smoked in baskets. Cooking seawater with coconut milk makes solid salt blocks, like the *túltul* of Guimaras. *Asín tibúok* of Bohol is moulded in a coconut shell. It is scraped off with a knife, often directly on cooked rice.

Atsára

/At·sá·ra/

Banana heart, unripe papaya, *dampálit* (samphire) leaf, carrot, white or pink ginger, red bell pepper, chili, garlic, and unripe mango are made into *atsára* (pickles). They can be soft or crisp, sometimes due to the use of lime powder but always steeped in vinegar, salt, and sugar. Pickles are eaten with fried dishes to cut the taste of fat.

Pangdagdág

/Pang·dag·dág/

Dagdag means "to supplement." The usual additions to sauces, dips, and mashes range from *wansúy* (coriander) leaves and tender tendrils of *pakó* (fiddlehead fern) to fine minced mixes of onion, garlic, shallot, and tomato. A seasonal treat is the addition of seaweed like *lató* (ar-arosép). The emergent combinations of robust diversity are a cross between a relish and a sálad.

Mga Sangkáp

/Sang·káp/

Ingredients

Philippine cuisine is a tribute to the natural surroundings and the societal memory that knows what is edible and not. Earliest foods were from shorelines and riversides: bivalves, fish, crustaceans, and seaweeds still eaten today. Low forests offered leaves, fruits, deer, birds, wild chicken and boar; Asian continental and insular botanicals like rice, mango, tamarind, and anise were added, Pacific-Asian coconut and taro. Ingredients originating in the Americas such as tomato, cacao, cashew, and turkey were brought by Spanish galleons beginning in the 16th century. European cow and wheat were introduced then, too. Contemporary Philippine cuisine knows no boundaries in what it uses to please the palate.

Mga Gulay

Vegetables

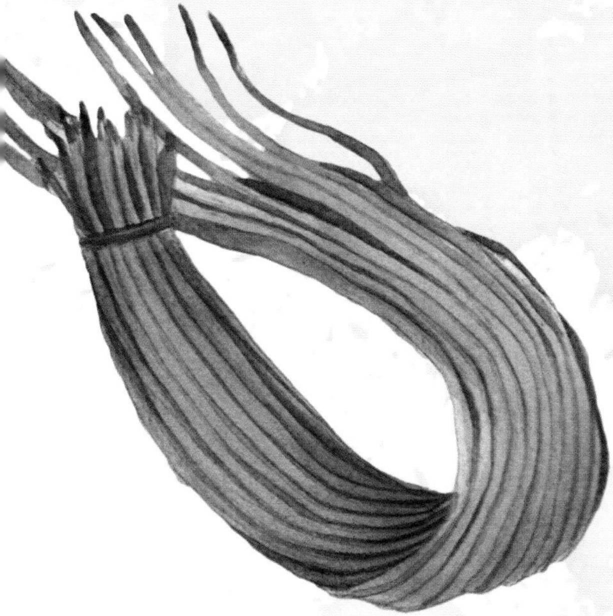

Sítaw /Sí·taw/
String Beans

Ampalayá /Am·pa·la·yá/
Bitter Gourd

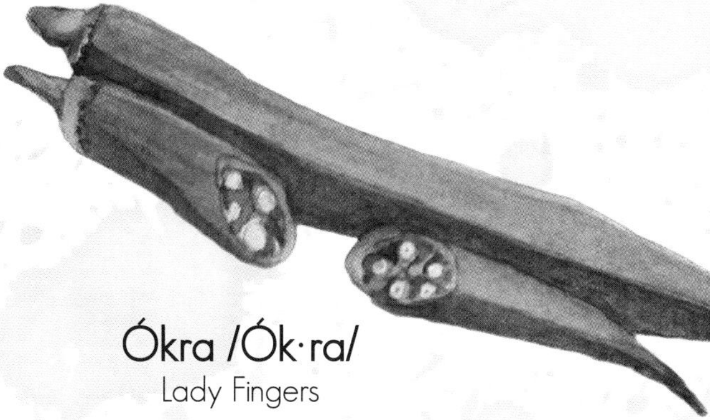

Ókra /Ók·ra/
Lady Fingers

Talóng /Ta·lóng/
Eggplant

Síling Pári /Sí·ling Pá·ri/

Bell Pepper

Repólyo /Re·pól·yo/

Cabbage

Sayóte /Sa·yó·te/

Chayote

Úpo /Ú·po/

Bottle Gourd

Péchay /Pé·chay/

Bok Choi

Károt /Ká·rot/

Carrot

Wansúy /Wan·súy/

Cilantro Leaves

Síling Labúyo /Sí·ling La·bu·yò/

Bird's Eye Chili

Maís /Ma·ís/

Corn

Báwang /Bá·wang/

Garlic

Lúya /Lú·ya/

Ginger

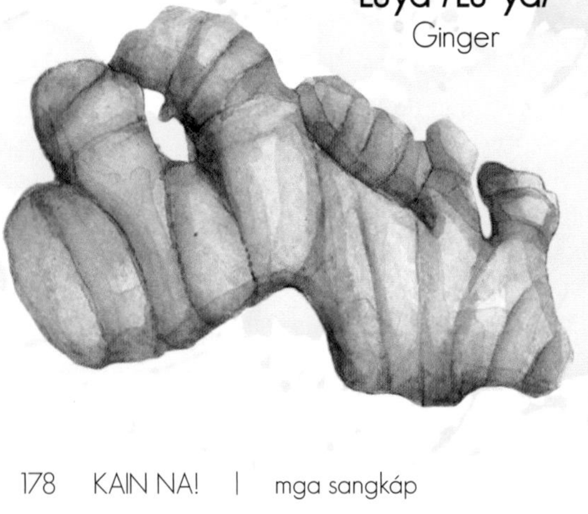

Pipíno /Pi·pí·no/

Cucumber

Singkamás /Sing·ka·más/
Jicama

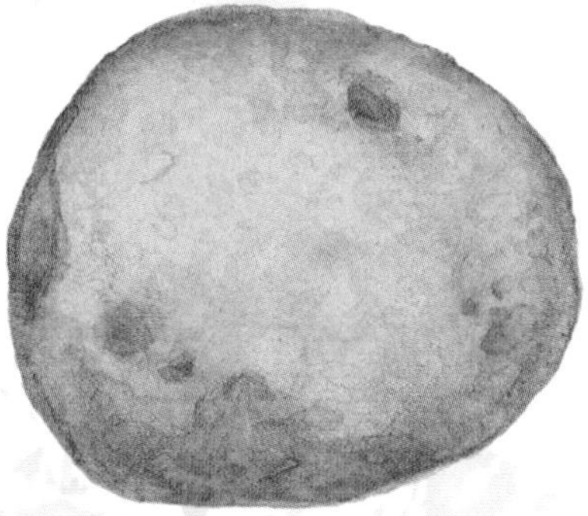

Patátas /Pa·tá·tas/
Potato

Tóge /Tó·ge/
Mung Bean Sprouts

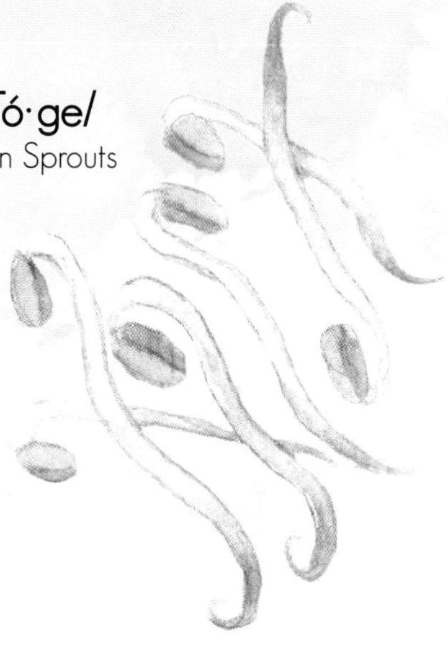

Sibúyas /Si·bú·yas/
Onion

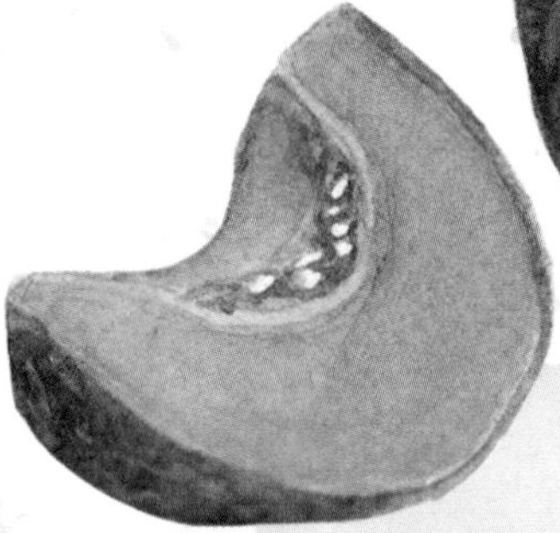
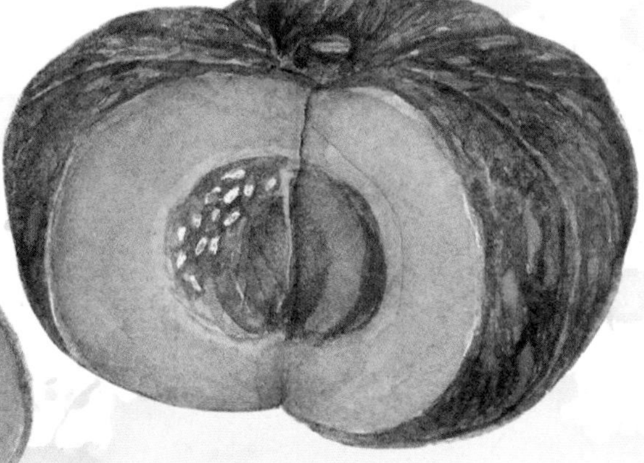

Kalabása /Ka·la·bá·sa/
Pumpkin

Patóla /Pa·tó·la/
Sponge Gourd

Alugbáti /A·lug·bá·ti/
Spinach

Labanós /La·ba·nós/
Radish

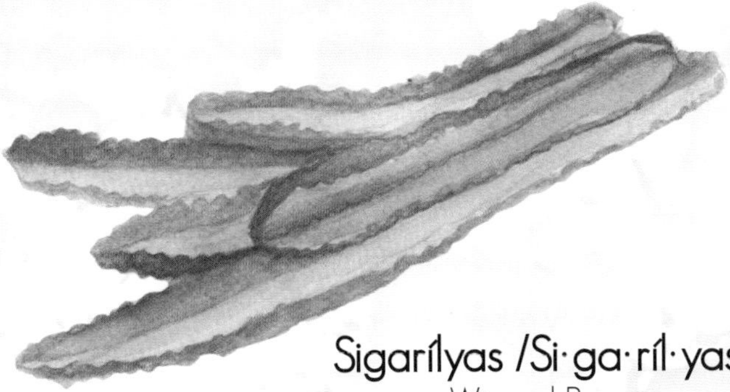

Sigarílyas /Si·ga·ríl·yas/
Winged Bean

Kangkóng /Kang·kóng/
Water Spinach

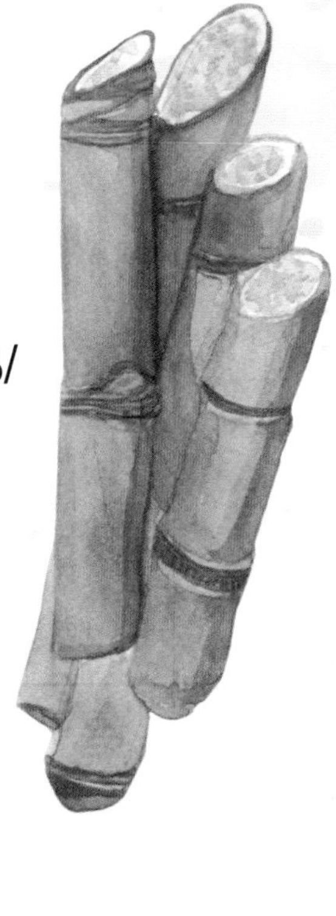

Tubó /Tu·bó/
Sugarcane

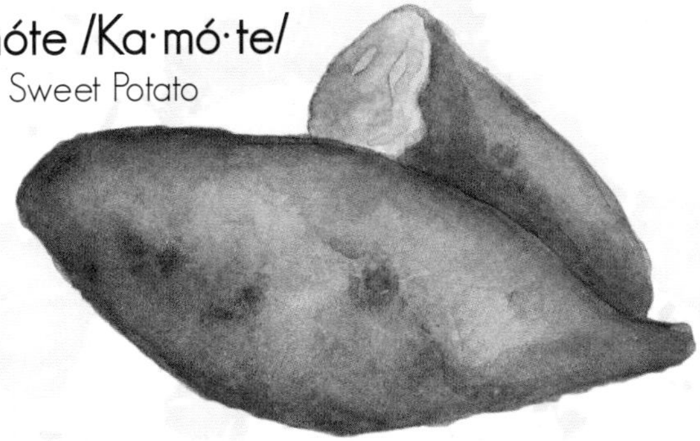

Kamóte /Ka·mó·te/
Sweet Potato

Malunggáy /Ma·lung·gáy/
Moringa Leaves

Púso ng Ságing /Pú·so ng Sá·ging/
Banana Blossom

Úbe /Ú·be/
Purple Yam

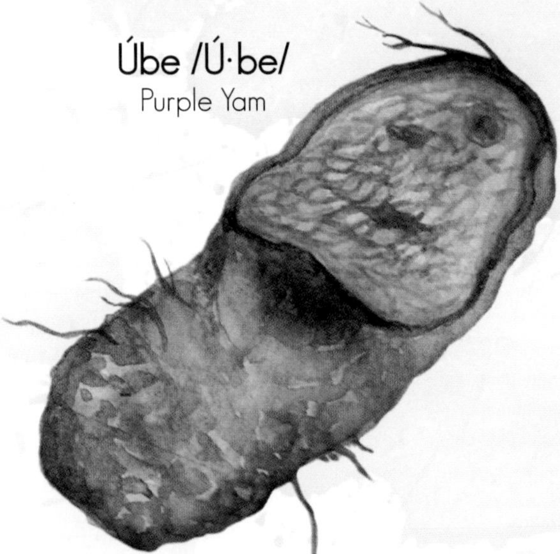

Niyóg /Ni·yóg/
Coconut Meat

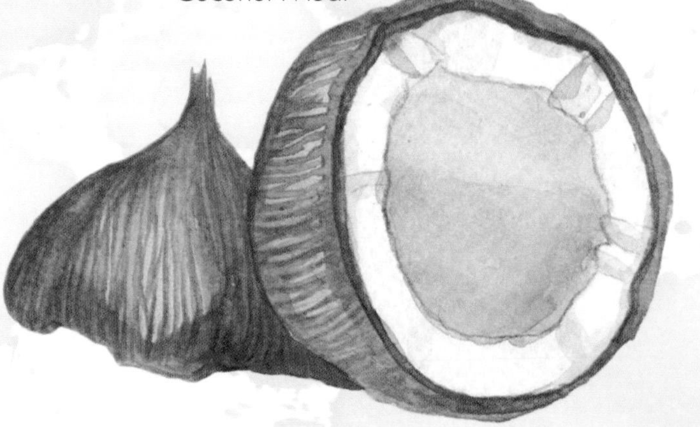

Lúyang Diláw /Lú·yang Di·láw/

Turmeric

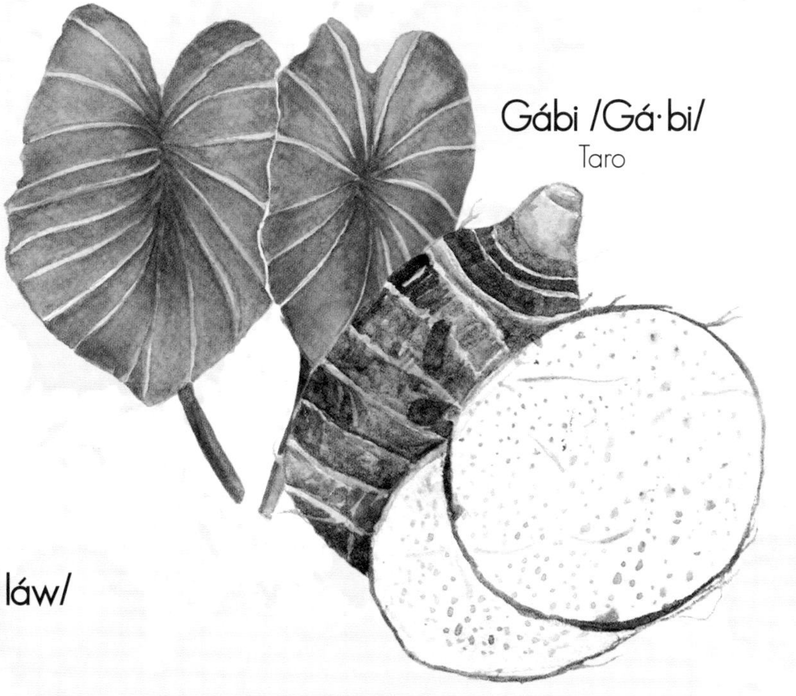

Gábi /Gá·bi/

Taro

Dáhon ng Mustásâ /Dá·hon ng Mus·tá·sâ/

Mustard Leaves

Sibúyas Tagálog /Si·bú·yas Ta·gá·log/

Shallots

Mga Prutas

Fruits

Abokádo /A·bo·ká·do/
Avocado

Ságing /Sá·ging/
Banana

Ságing na Sabá /Sá·ging na Sa·bá/
Saba Banana

Mansánas /Man·sá·nas/
Apple

Bayábas /Ba·yá·bas/
Guava

Suhà /Su·hà/
Pomelo

Búko /Bú·ko/
Coconut

Úbas /Ú·bas/
Grapes

Langkâ /Lang·kâ/
Jackfruit

Kamyás /Kam·yás/
Bilimbi

Dáyap /Dá·yap/
Lime

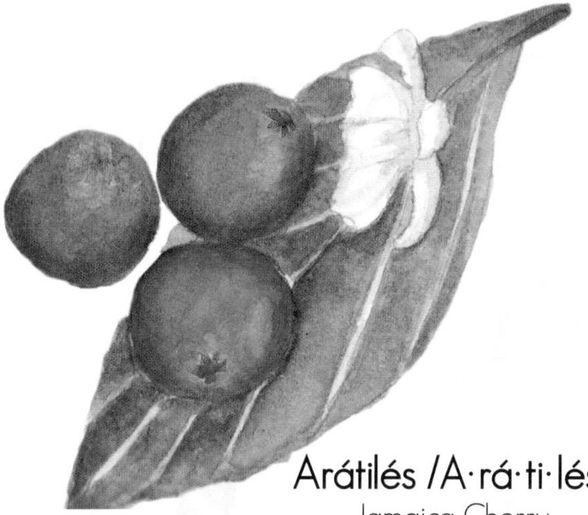

Arátilés /A·rá·ti·lés/
Jamaica Cherry

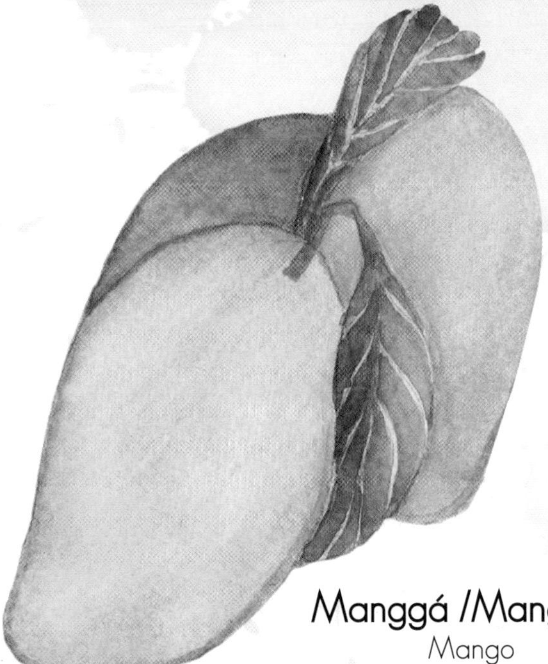

Manggá /Mang·gá/
Mango

Dalandán /Da·lan·dán/
Native Lemon

Dúhat /Du·hat/
Native Blackberry

Kamátis /Ka·má·tis/

Tomato

Pinyá /Pin·yá/

Pineapple

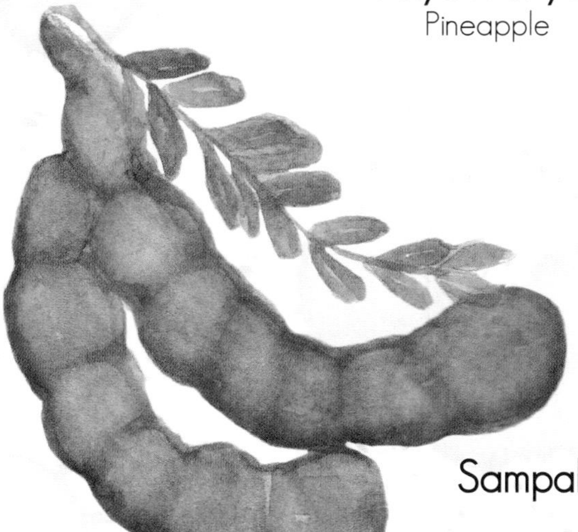

Sampalok /Sam·pá·lok/

Tamarind

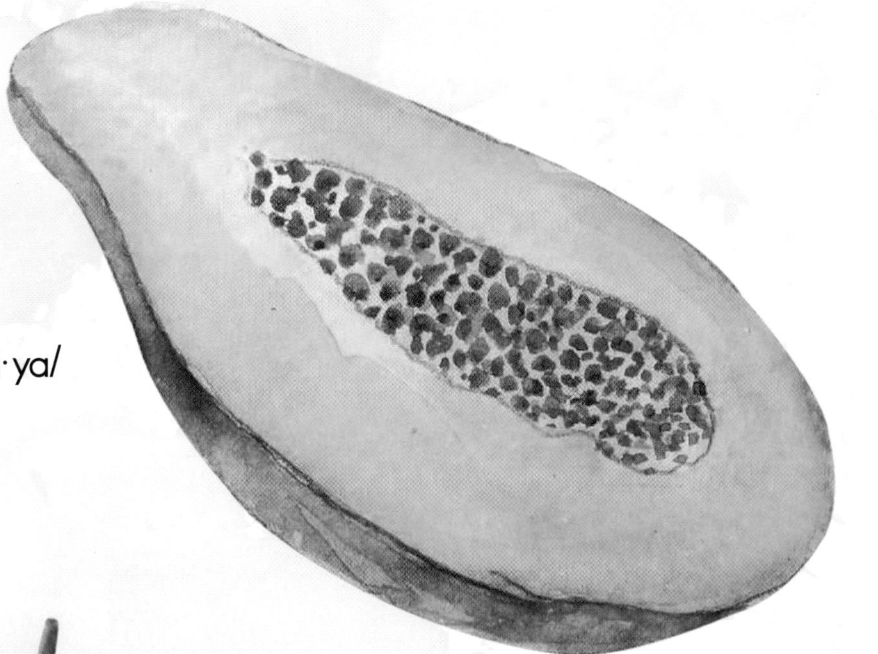

Papáya /Pa·pá·ya/
Papaya

Dalanghíta /Da·lang·hí·ta/
Mandarin Orange

Átis /Á·tis/
Sugar Apple

Kalamansí /Ka·la·man·sí/
Calamansi

Pakwán /Pak·wán/
Watermelon

Karne at Lamang Dagat

Meat & Seafood

Bangús /Ba·ngús/
Milkfish

Báka /Bá·ka/
Beef

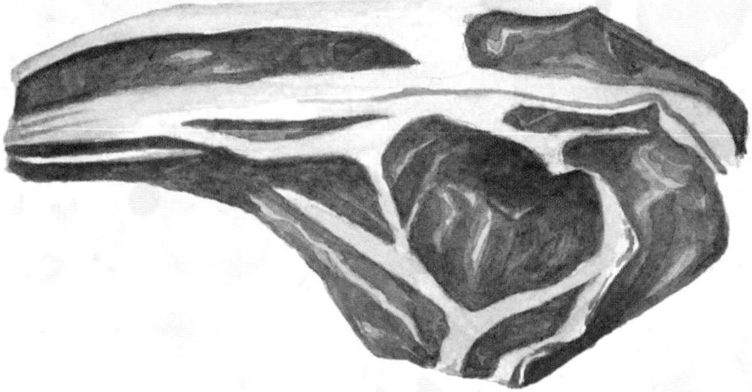

Galúnggong /Ga·lúng·gong/
Mackarel

Hípon /Hí·pon/

Shrimp

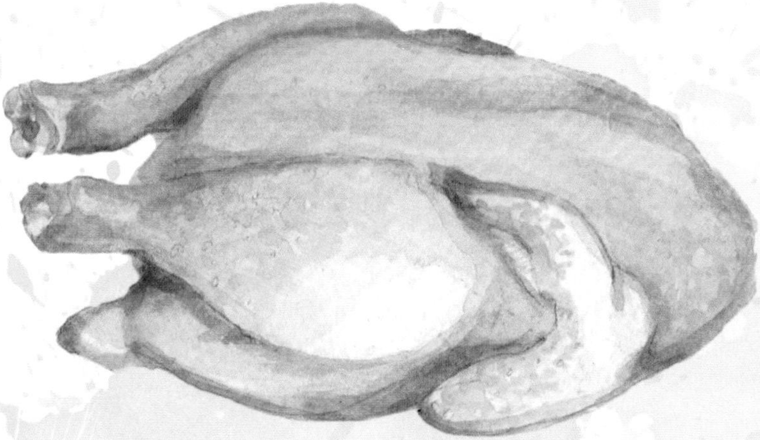

Manók /Ma·nók/

Chicken

Báboy /Bá·boy/

Pork

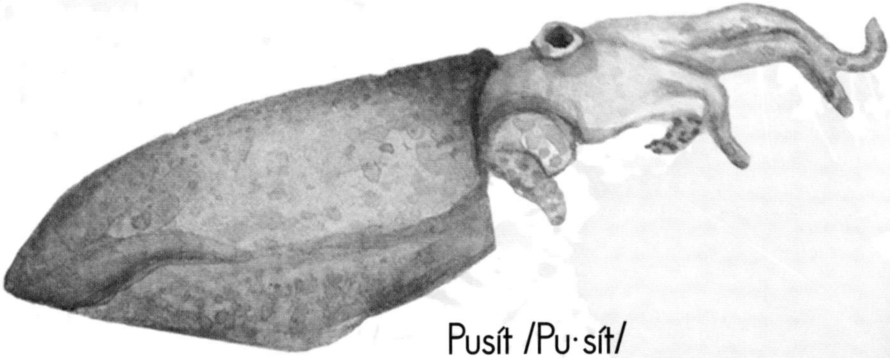

Pusít /Pu·sít/
Squid

Tahóng /Ta·hóng/
Mussels

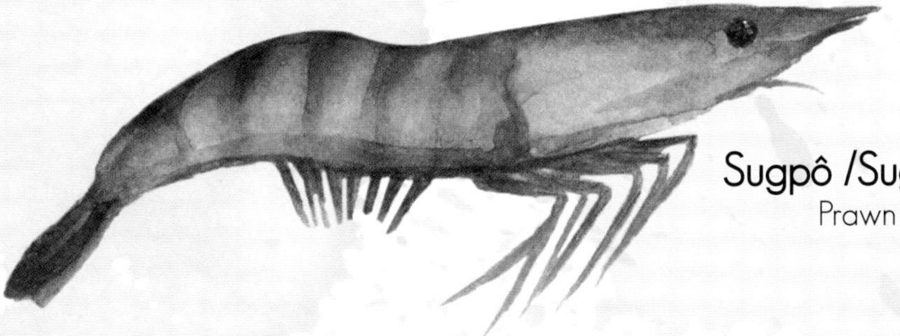

Sugpô /Sug·pô/
Prawn

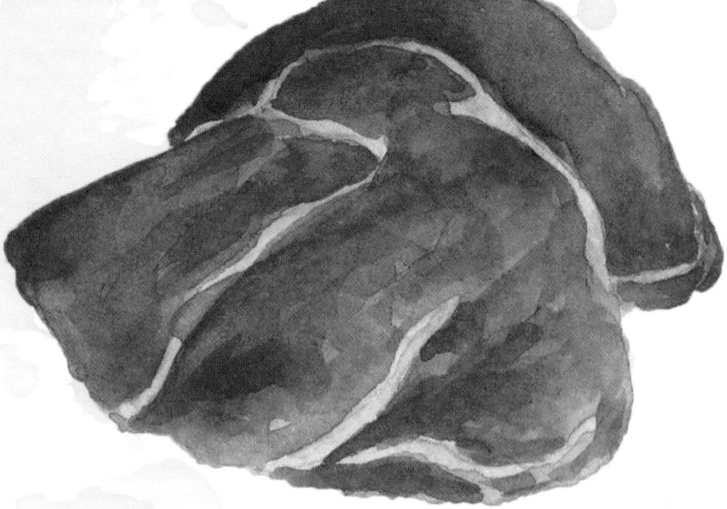

Kalabáw /Ka·la·báw/
Water Buffalo

Lápu-Lápu /Lá·pu-Lá·pu/
Grouper

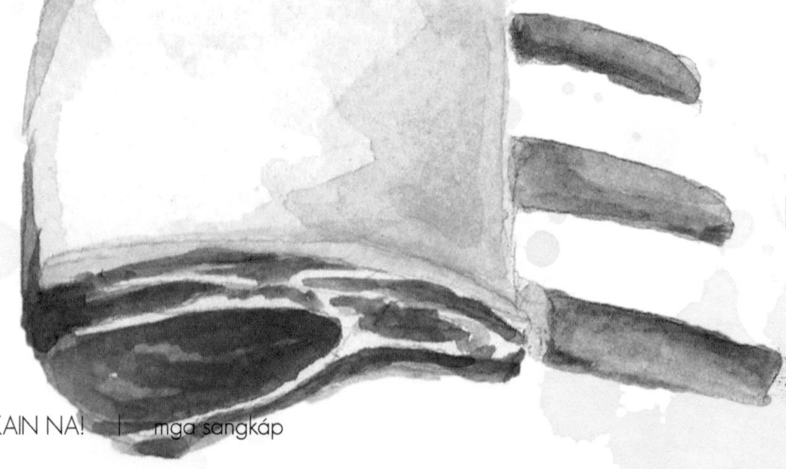

Kambíng /Kam·bíng/
Goat

Alimángo /A·li·má·ngo/
Pond Crab

Alimásag /A·li·má·sag/
Sea Crab

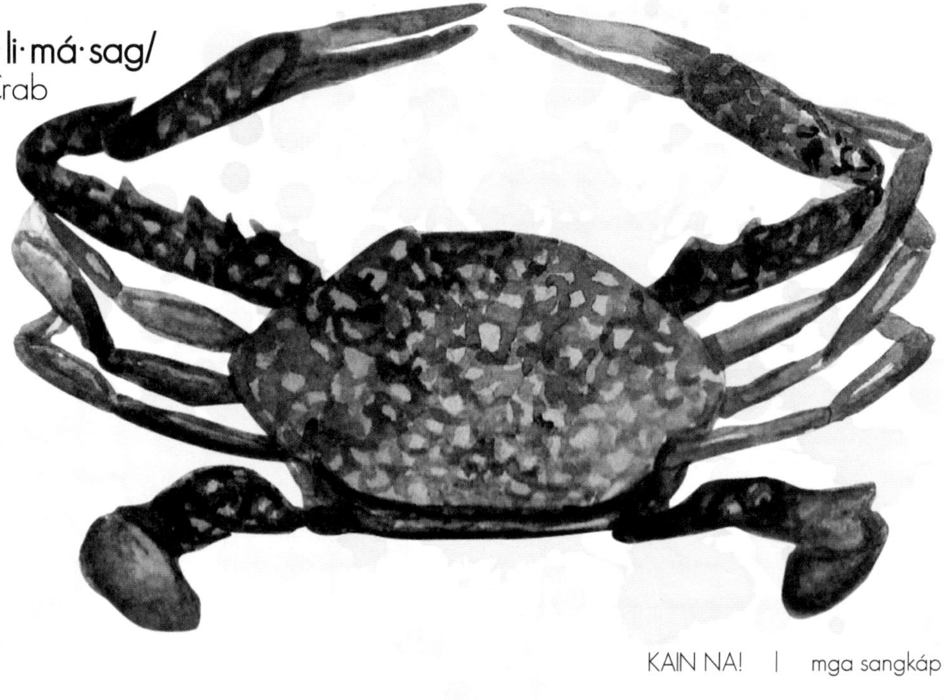

Talabá /Ta·la·bá/
Oysters

Tinapá /Ti·na·pá/
Smoked Fish

Halaán /Ha·la·án/

Clams

At Ibá Pá

and others

Asín /A·sín/
Salt

Gatâ /Ga·tâ/
Coconut Milk

Pamintá /Pa·min·tá/
Pepper

Asúkal /A·sú·kal/
Sugar

Tóyo /Tó·yo/
Soy Sauce

Patís /Pa·tís/
Fish or Shrimp Sauce

Súka /Sú·ka/

Vinegar

Atsuwéte /At·su·wé·te/

Annatto Seeds

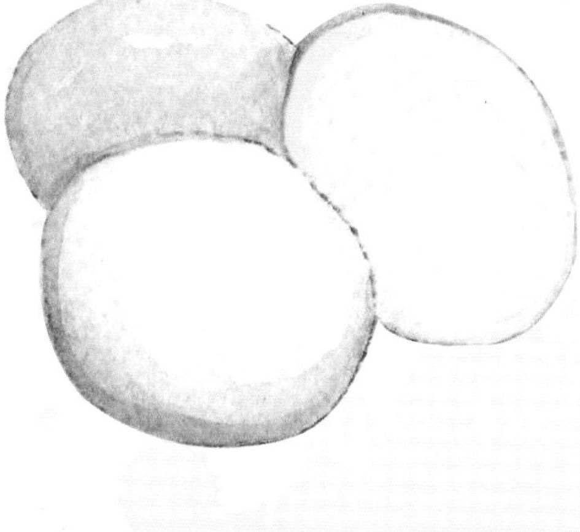

Itlog /It·lóg/

Egg

Itlóg ng Púgo /It·lóg ng Pú·go/

Quail Egg

Dáhon ng Lawrél /Dá·hon ng Law·rél/

Bayleaf

Itlóg na Pulá /It·lóg na Pu·lá/

Red Eggs

Bigás /Bi·gás/
Uncooked Rice

Sáing or Kánin /Sá·ing/ or /Ká·nin/
Cooked Rice

Kasubhâ /Ka·sub·hâ/
Safflower

Bagoóng /Ba·go·óng/
Fish or Shrimp Paste

Gátas /Gá·tas/
Milk

Késo /Ké·so/
Cheese

Dáhon ng Ságing /Dá·hon ng Sá·ging/
Banana Leaf

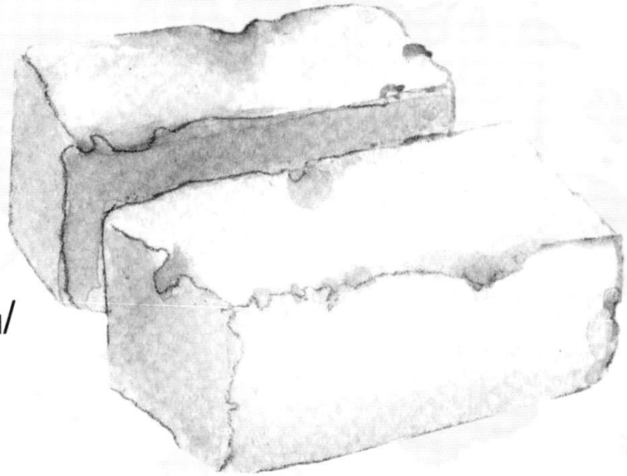

Tókwa /Tók·wa/
Tofu

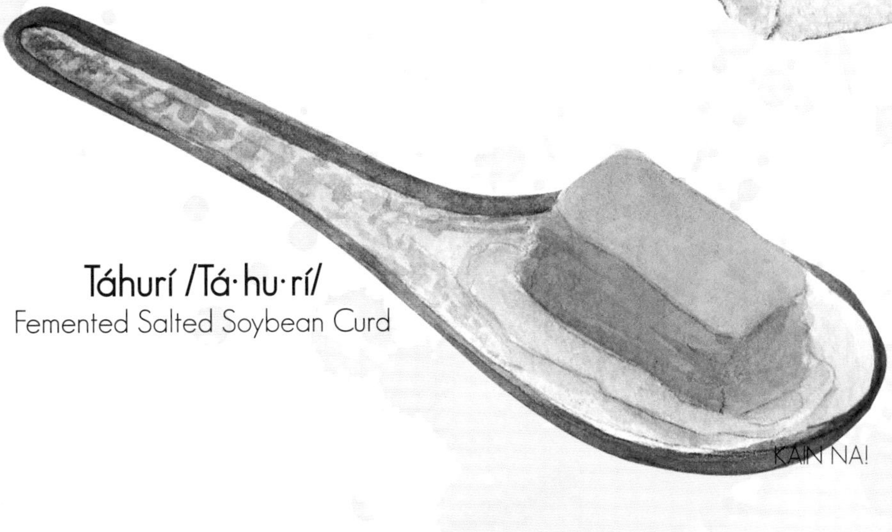

Táhurí /Tá·hu·rí/
Femented Salted Soybean Curd

Butó ng Lingá /Bu·tó ng Li·ngá/
Sesame Seeds

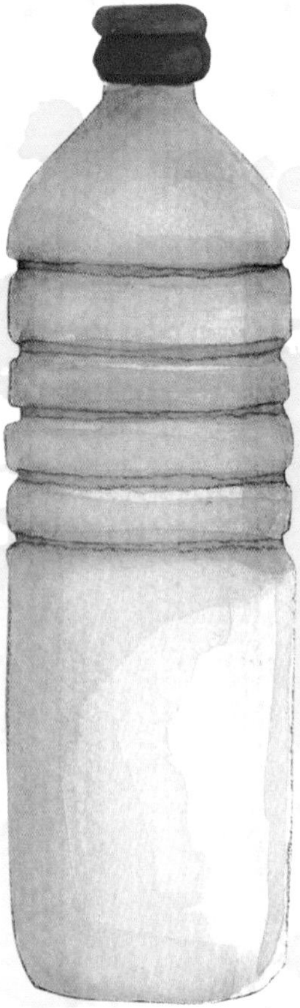

Langís ng Niyóg /La·ngís ng Ni·yóg/
Coconut Oil

Anis /A·nís/
Star Anise

Fresh Chinese Noodles

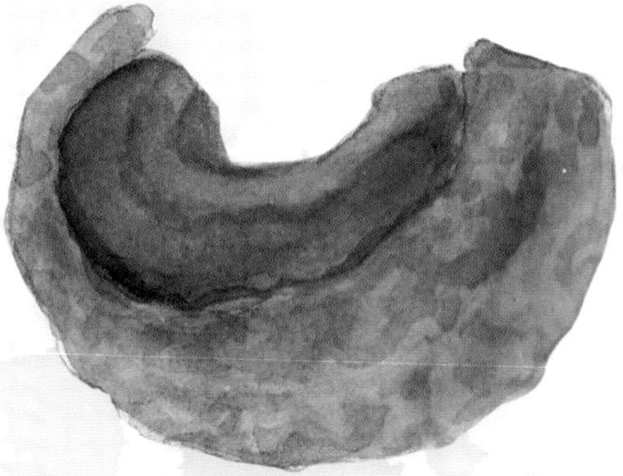

Chicharón /Chi·cha·rón/

Crackling

Krópek /Kró·pek/

Fried Cracker

Acknowledgements

The publisher, authors, and illustrator would like to thank the following for their support in the production of this book:

Renan Prado, *Michaela Fenix*, *Ana Urbina*, *Jomar Cañega*, *Alpha Garcia*, *Vin Basilio*, *FJ Hicban*, *Ana Lopez-Gray*, *Tiffany Jillian Go*, and *Asia Society Philippines*

This book would not have been possible without each and every one of you.

Káin Ná!

About the Authors

FELICE PRUDENTE STA. MARIA is a pioneer of Philippine culinary history. She uses a polychronic and multidisciplinary framework for establishing culinary history with focus on the period of 1516 to 1949. The Governor-General's Kitchen: Philippine Culinary Vignettes and Recipes, 1521-1935 (Anvil Publishing, 2006 and 2011) and What Kids Should Know About Philippine Food (Adarna Books, 2016) are among her popular works. Her writings about Philippine culture over four decades have been awarded both nationally and internationally. In the 1980s she received the first Kalakbay Award from the Philippine Department of Tourism in the Domestic Resident Travel Writer category. In 2001, she was added to the SEA Write Award roster, considered the highest accolade for ASEAN authors. Sta. Maria continues to speak on the value of culinary history for tourism to professional and academic audiences.

BRYAN KOH released his first book, Milk Pigs & Violet Gold: Philippine Cookery in 2014. It won the Best Food Book Award at the Philippine National Book Awards that year. His second book, 0451 Mornings are for Mont Hin Gar: Burmese Food Stories won third place in the Best Asian Cookbook category at the World Gourmand Cookbook Awards 2016. Milk Pigs' second, enriched, edition, entitled Milkier Pigs & Violet Gold, was nominated for Best Travel Food Book at the World Gourmand Cookbook Awards 2017. He released his third book, Bekwoh, on the cuisine of Peninsular Malaysia's East Coast, in 2018. Bryan majored in Mathematics at the National University of Singapore and has a Masters in Management Hospitality from Cornell University. He lives in Singapore and is co-owner of cake companies Chalk Farm and Milk Moons.

About the Illustrator

MARIEL YLAGAN GARCIA is an illustrator/painter based in the Philippines, who specializes in watercolor and oil painting. Realizing her artistic skills at 10, her love and passion for the creative medium became key drivers to pursuing that journey full time, beginning with finishing Multimedia Arts at Malayan Colleges Laguna in 2015. Most of her works are inspired by botanical and female figures. Mariel is a member of the Kapisanan ng mga Pintor sa Pilipinas at iba pang Sining. Inc. (KPP) and Space 4026 where she explores, shares and exhibits her art. In 2014, she started an internship at Ayala Museum wherein she designed event posters, organized exhibits and assisted art workshops. Mariel continues to paint and now exhibits around the Metro.